The TWELVE

A Perpetual Calendar

Illustrated by
ARMIN LANDECK

The Twelve Seasons

A Perpetual Calendar
for the Country

Joseph Wood Krutch

SEASONS

for the Country

WILLIAM SLOANE ASSOCIATES

Publishers   *New York*

Third Printing, August 1965

Manufactured in the United States of America

A26-2

For MARCELLE

who will be found between the lines

CONTENTS

CONTENTS

April

The Day of the Peepers

Hyla crucifer is what the biologists call him, but to most of us he is simply the Spring Peeper. The popularizers of natural history have by no means neglected him but even without their aid he has made himself known to many whose only wild flower is the daisy and whose only bird is the robin. Everyone who has ever visited the country in the spring has heard him trilling from the marsh at twilight, and though few have ever caught sight of him most know that he is a little, inch-long frog who has just awaked from his winter sleep. In southern Connecticut he usually begins to pipe on some day between the middle of March and the middle of April, and I, like most country dwellers, listen for the first of his shrill, cold notes.

Throughout the winter, neighbors who met in the village street have been greeting one another with the conventional question: "Is it cold enough for you?" Or, perhaps, if they are of the type which watches a bit more carefully than most the phenomenon of the seasons, they have been comparing thermometers in the hope that someone will admit to a minimum at least one degree higher than what was recorded "over my way." Now, however, one announces triumphantly: "Heard the peepers last night," and the other goes home to tell his wife. Few are High Church enough to risk a "Christ is risen" on Easter morning, but the peepers are mentioned without undue self-consciousness.

Even this, however, is not enough for me and I have often wondered that a world which pretends to mark so many days and to celebrate so many occasions should accept quite so casually the day when *Hyla crucifer* announces that winter is over. One swallow does not make a spring, and the robin arrives with all the philistine unconcern of a worldling back from his Winter at Aiken or Palm Beach. But the peeper seems to realize, rather better than we, the significance of his resurrection, and I wonder if there is any other phenomenon in the heavens above or in the earth beneath which so simply and so definitely announces that life is resurgent again.

April

We who have kept artificially warm and active through the winter act as though we were really independent of the seasons, but we forget how brief our immunity is and are less anxious than we might be if habit had not dulled our awareness. One summer which failed to arrive and we should realize well enough before we perished of hunger that we are only a little less at the mercy of the seasons than the weed that dies in October. One winter which lasted not six months but twelve and we should recognize our affinity with the insects who give up the ghost after laying the eggs that would never hatch if they did not lie chill and dead through the cold of a winter as necessary to them as warmth was to the males who fertilized and the females who laid them. We waited through the long period during which our accumulated supplies of food grew smaller and we waited calmly in a blind assurance that warmth would return and that nature would reawaken. Now, the voice of the peeper from the marsh announces the tremendous fact that our faith has been justified. A sigh of relief should go up and men should look at one another with a wild surprise. "It" has happened again, though there was nothing during the long months that passed to support our conviction that it could and would.

We had, to be sure, the waiting pages of our calendars marked "June," "July," and even, of all things, "August." The sun, so the astronomers had assured us, had turned northward on a certain date and theoretically had been growing stronger day by day. But there was, often enough, little in the mercury of our thermometers or the feel of our fingers to confirm the fact. Many a March day had felt colder than the milder days of February. And merely astronomical seasons have, after all, very little relation to any actual human experience either as visible phenomena or as events bringing with them concomitant earthly effects.

Not one man out of a hundred thousand would be aware of the solstices or the equinoxes if he did not see their dates set down in the almanac or did not read about them in the newspaper. They cannot be determined without accurate instruments and they correspond to no phenomena he is aware of. But the year as we live it does have its procession of recurring events, and it is a curious commentary on the extent to which we live by mere symbols that ten men know that the spring equinox occurs near the twenty-first of March to one who could give you even the approximate date when the peepers begin in his community; and that remains true even if he happens to be a countryman and even if he usually remarks, year after year, when they do begin.

It is true that the Day of the Peepers is a movable feast. But so is Easter, which—as a matter of fact—can come earlier or later by just about the same number of days that, on the calendar I have kept, separates the earliest from the latest date upon which *Hyla crucifer* begins to call. Moreover, the earliness or the lateness of the peepers means something, as the earliness or the lateness of Easter does not.

Whatever the stars may say or whatever the sun's altitude may be, spring has not begun until the ice has melted and life begun to stir again. Your peeper makes a calculation which would baffle a meteorologist. He takes into consideration the maximum to which the temperature has risen, the minimum to which it has fallen during the night, the relative length of the warmer and the colder periods, besides, no doubt, other factors hard to get down in tables or charts. But at last he knows that the moment has come. It has been just warm enough just long enough, and without too much cold in between. He inflates the little bubble in his throat and sends out the clear note audible for half a mile. On that day something older than any Christian God has risen. The earth is alive again.

The human tendency to prefer abstractions to phenomena is, I know, a very ancient one. Some anthropologists, noting that abstract design seems usually to come before the pictorial representation of anything in primitive man's environment, have said that the first picture drawn by any beginning culture is a picture of God. Certainly in the European world astronomy was the first of the sciences, and it is curious to remember that men knew a great deal about the intricate dance

of the heavenly bodies before they had so much as noticed the phenomena of life about them. The constel-
lations were named before any except the most obvious
animals or plants and were studied before a science of
botany or physiology had begun. The Greeks, who
thought that bees were generated in the carcasses of
dead animals and that swallows hibernated under the
water, could predict eclipses, and the very Druids were
concerned to mark the day on which the sun turned
northward again. But the earliest of the sciences is also
the most remote and the most abstract. The objects
with which it deals are not living things and its crucial
events do not correspond directly or immediately to
any phenomena which are crucial in the procession of
events as they affect animal or vegetable life.

Easter is an anniversary, and the conception of an
anniversary is not only abstract but so difficult to define
that the attempt to fix Easter used up an appalling proportion of the mental energy of learned men for many
hundreds of years—ultimately to result in nothing except a cumbersome complexity that is absolutely meaningless in the end. Why should we celebrate the first
Sunday after the first full moon on or after the twenty-
first of March? What possible meaning can the result
of such a calculation have? Yet even that meaningless
definition of Easter is not really accurate. For the purpose of determining the festival, the date of the full
moon is assumed to be, not that of the actual full moon,

but that on which the full moon would have fallen if the table worked out by Pope Gregory's learned men had been—as it is not—really accurate. Even the relatively few men who remember the commonly given formula will occasionally find that they have missed their attempt to determine when Easter will be because they consulted a lay calendar to find the full moon instead of concerning themselves with the Epact and considering the theoretical ecclesiastical full moon rather than the actual one. How much easier it is to celebrate the Day of the Peepers instead, and how much more meaningful too! On that day something miraculous and full of promise has actually happened, and that something announces itself in no uncertain terms.

Over any astronomically determined festival, the Day of the Peepers has, moreover, another advantage even greater than the simplicity with which it defines itself or the actuality of its relation to the season it announces, for *Hyla crucifer* is a sentient creature who shares with us the drama and the exultation; who, indeed, sings our hosannahs for us. The music of the spheres is a myth; to say that the heavens rejoice is a pathetic fallacy; but there is no missing the rejoicings from the marsh and no denying that they are something shared. Under the stars we feel alone but by the pond side we have company.

To most, to be sure, Hyla is a *vox et praterea nihil.* Out of a thousand who have heard him, hardly one has ever seen him at the time of his singing or recognized him if perchance he has happened by pure accident to see squatting on the branch of some shrub the tiny inch-long creature, gray or green according to his mood, and with a dark cross over his back. But it was this tiny creature who, some months before, had congregated with his fellows in the cold winter to sing and make love. No one could possibly humanize him as one humanizes a pet and so come to feel that he belongs to us rather than—what is infinitely more important—that we both, equally, belong to something more inclusive than ourselves.

Like all the reptiles and the amphibians he has an aspect which is inscrutable and antediluvian. His thoughts must be inconceivably different from ours and his joy hardly less so. But the fact is comforting rather than the reverse, for if we are nevertheless somehow united with him in that vast category of living things which is so sharply cut off from everything that does not live at all, then we realize how broad the base of the category is, how much besides ourselves is, as it were, on our side. Over against the atoms and the stars are set both men and frogs. Life is not something entrenched in man alone, in a creature who has not been here so very long and may not continue to be here so very much longer. We are not its sole guardians, not alone in enjoying or enduring it. It is not something that will fail if we should.

Strangely enough, however, man's development takes him farther and farther away from association with his fellows, seems to condemn him more and more to live with what is dead rather than with what is alive. It is not merely that he dwells in cities and associates with machines rather than with plants and with animals. That, indeed, is but a small and a relatively unimportant part of his growing isolation. Far more important is the fact that more and more he thinks in terms of abstractions, generalizations, and laws; less and less participates in the experience of living in a world of sights, and sounds, and natural urges.

Electricity, the most powerful of his servants, flows silently and invisibly. It isn't really there except in its effects. We plan our greatest works on paper and in adding machines. Push the button, turn the switch! Things happen. But they are things we know about only in terms of symbols and formulae. Do we inevitably, in the process, come ourselves to be more and more like the inanimate forces with which we deal, less and less like the animals among whom we arose? Yet it is of protoplasm that we are made. We cannot possibly become like atoms or like suns. Do we dare to forget as completely as we threaten to forget that we belong rejoicing by the marsh more anciently and more fundamentally than we belong by the machine or over the drawing board?

No doubt astronomy especially fascinated the first

men who began to think because the world in which they lived was predominantly so immediate and so confused a thing, was composed so largely of phenomena which they could see and hear but could not understand or predict and to which they so easily fell victim. The night sky spread out above them defined itself clearly and exhibited a relatively simple pattern of surely recurring events. They could perceive an order and impose a scheme, thus satisfying an intellectual need to which the natural phenomena close about them refused to cater.

But the situation of modern man is exactly the reverse. He "understands" more and more as he sees and hears less and less. By the time he has reached high-school age he has been introduced to the paradox that the chair on which he sits is not the hard object it seems to be but a collection of dancing molecules. He learns to deal, not with objects but with statistics, and before long he is introduced to the idea that God is a mathematician, not the creator of things seen, and heard, and felt. As he is taught to trust less and less the evidence of the five senses with which he was born, he lives less and less in the world which they seem to reveal, more and more with the concepts of physics and biology. Even his body is no longer most importantly the organs and muscles of which he is aware but the hormones of which he is told.

The very works of art that he looks at when he seeks

delight through the senses are no longer representations of what the eye has seen but constructions and designs —or, in other words, another order of abstractions. It is no wonder that for such a one spring should come, not when the peepers begin, but when the sun crosses the equator or rather—since that is only a human interpretation of the phenomenon—when the inclined axis of the earth is for an instant pointed neither toward nor away from the sun but out into space in such a way that it permits the sun's rays to fall upon all parts of the earth's surface for an equal length of time. For him astronomy does not, as it did for primitive man, represent the one successful attempt to intellectualize and render abstract a series of natural phenomena. It is, instead, merely one more of the many systems by which understanding is substituted for experience.

Surely one day a year might be set aside on which to celebrate our ancient loyalties and to remember our ancient origins. And I know of none more suitable for that purpose than the Day of the Peepers. "Spring is come!", I say when I hear them, and: "The most ancient of Christs has risen!" But I also add something which, for me at least, is even more important. "Don't forget," I whisper to the peepers; "we are all in this together."

May

A Question for Meloë

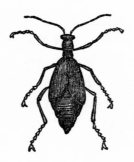

At some moment when my back was turned the Connecticut spring slipped up on me again. As usual I had noted the grosser, more publicized phenomena as they appeared in their expected order. The first sound of the peepers and the first appearance of a fox sparrow were duly noted in my diary. So too was the blooming of the hepatica and, in the little wood pools, the appearance of feathery-gilled tadpoles hatched from eggs laid by a salamander a few weeks before.

But it is not these things that really change the landscape and give the whole world a new look. We await them eagerly because we know that they are points of reference; that by them we can gauge the advance of the season. But there are a thousand other phenomena

no less important and far more elusive—the slow green-
ing of the grass and the slow appearance from the
ground of the thousands upon thousands of weeds and
flowers.

Your peeper is either singing or he isn't; your fox
sparrow is either there or not there. But who can say
that he ever saw a blade of grass come up out of the
ground, much less that he ever saw one of the spears
which survived the winter turn green? These things
do nevertheless happen, and suddenly one is aware
that they have happened.

Again and again I have resolved that I would catch
them at it, or at least be able to say: "Yesterday the
grass looked as it has looked ever since the snow left;
today it is different." But, as usual, I missed this as I
missed all the other important things. Suddenly I realized that the world no longer looked as it had looked
ten days ago. But when did the thing happen? Was it
during yesterday, or during last night? Or was it perhaps three days or three nights ago? I cannot, alas,
answer that question though no one, I am sure, would
like better than I to be able to do so.

So many different things have responded almost si-
multaneously to warmth and moisture that it is difficult
not to think of them as to some extent co-operating,
one with another; of putting on some sort of co-ordi-
nated show for the benefit of the spectator. The image
that comes most immediately to mind is the image of

a magician waving his wand or, perhaps, a conductor his baton. Each performer seems to know his part and eagerly to make his contribution.

But so pretty a picture is purely fanciful. Every tree, every bird, every blade of grass, is fiercely individualistic. It springs to life, not in order to make its contribution to a pageant, but in order not to be left behind in the struggle for water, and sun, and the few cubic centimeters of soil which this year it will contest not only with the roots of the neighboring plantlet—which last summer it fought to a draw—but also with the new seeds dropped perhaps as autumn drew to a close. Murder will be done this spring in the woods, on my lawn, and even in the crannies of my garden wall.

A great many people have been impressed by the orderliness of Nature, but if by nature is meant the aggregate of living things, then I must confess that her untidiness is what has most often struck me. As a countryman who just barely escapes the shame of suburbanity, I have struggled almost as much as the suburbanite does against summer's disorderly profusion and against autumn's messy habit of scattering leaves where they least ought to be. However, I am willing to admit that all this is significant only when seen from the standpoint of a very late comer into the universe whose fussy little preferences are of no great importance; and it is not what I really mean when I say that Nature does not seem to operate in accordance with any well-thought-

May

out scheme of her own; that hers is not, if I may put it this way, a planned economy.

I can understand how an astronomer may conclude that God is a mathematician. The planets seem to know where they are going and what they are about. Theirs is a formal, unvarying dance which moves in accord with an abstract scheme of delightful regularity; and the mathematical physicist seems to have discovered that the microcosm is, despite the disturbing presence of certain principles suggesting indeterminacy, a good deal like its big brother the system of heavenly bodies. But the world of living things exhibits no such co-operation of part with part, no such subordination of the unit to the whole. The God who planned the well-working machines which function as atom and solar system seems to have had no part in arranging the curiously inefficient society of plants and animals in which everything works against everything else; and the struggle between, let us say, the mouse which would continue its species and the owl which would feed its young goes on inconclusively millennium after millennium.

No one, it seems to me, who has ever watched the contest between two weeds for a few square inches of soil; no one who has seen all the intricate history of the one, from seed to leaf, come to nothing—can possibly suppose that so wasteful a game of cross-purposes was deliberately devised by the astronomer's mathematical

God, or indeed by any intelligence which knew what it wanted. If a God made the world of atoms and suns, then perhaps life intruded itself unexpectedly to impose, through some will of its own, multiplicity upon unity, disorder upon order, conflict upon balance. The individual plant or animal is no doubt marvelously contrived to achieve its purposes, but the society of living things is an anarchy in which events may work themselves out to this conclusion or that—but over which no unity of purpose seems to preside.

Before the summer is far advanced I shall probably some day see crawling along at my feet a small beetle, blue-black and shiny, whose oversized abdomen seems rather repulsively too big for wing cases which cannot quite cover it as those of trimmer beetles do. It will be a member of the genus Meloë, some of whom act out life histories astonishingly complex and grotesquely improbable even for a member of the insect clan, many species of which go in for improbable habits. When I see our American Meloë, I am always reminded of Henri Fabre's account, read many years ago, of his research into the history of a species of Meloë common in the south of France. What he discovered will strike me again as perhaps the most apt illustration of what I have just been trying to suggest—namely, the lack of intelligent planning in the scheme which has gradually worked itself out in living nature.

May

Anyone who cares to do so may read the full, fascinating, almost insane story in the second volume of the *Souvenirs Entomologiques*. Reduced to its barest outline, what happens is approximately this: Meloë lays a prodigious number of eggs—perhaps ten or twelve thousand. They hatch into strange little creatures looking like small lice, and these small creatures climb up the stalks of flowers where they wait patiently for the chance that some flying insect may pass by. The lucky ones are rewarded. They proceed immediately to climb aboard the visitor and to hide themselves among the downy hairs with which most flying insects are covered. It was there, by the way, that Linnaeus knew they were to be found, and because of that fact he named them *Pediculus apis*, or bee-louse, never suspecting that they were merely the immature form of a beetle having a name of its own.

Now presumably a considerable proportion of Meloë's ten thousand children die for the simple reason that no flying insect comes near enough for them to mount. They perish like some unsuccessful hitch-hiker whose whole intellectual equipment consists in the instinct to hold up a thumb and who can do nothing except perish of starvation if no one stops soon enough to give him a lift. But this is only the beginning of the infant Meloë's usually catastrophic history. Most of those who do succeed in stealing a ride have simply reached another dead-end. They die on an insect's back instead of on a flower stem.

By pure chance, however, some few will happen to find themselves on the back of a mason bee of the genus Anthophora. These lucky ones will ultimately be carried to the nest of the Anthophore who has prepared a little pool of honey destined to nourish one of her own offspring to be hatched from an egg set afloat on the pool. Baby Meloë would drown in the honey itself, but he waits until the Anthophore's egg is being laid, slips from the insect onto the egg, and then floats with it upon the surface of the honey. He now begins to nourish himself upon the bee's egg and, before the raft to which he is clinging is completely consumed, he transforms himself into a second larval form capable of surviving in the honey pool itself. Finally, to cut the long story short, he becomes an adult Meloë, ready to start the whole absurd business over again.

I do not suppose that Lewis Carroll ever heard of Meloë, but Meloë's history reminds one of that strange insect the Bread-and-butter-fly which, so Alice was told, lived on weak tea with cream in it. "Supposing it couldn't find any?" Alice asked. "Then it would die, of course." "But that must happen very often." "It always happens." The only difference is that it does not quite always happen to Meloë. All the fortuitous circumstances necessary for his survival do sometimes present themselves. Improbable as it may seem, there are plenty of Meloës about. If we assume that their number is neither increasing nor decreasing and that ten thousand is the average number of eggs laid, then just once in five thousand instances all the improbable things do happen. The system, we see, does work. But it does not seem a very sensible one. Even most insects have found simpler ways of reproducing themselves.

Fabre, devout Catholic and sturdy antievolutionist that he was, seems to imply that the case of Meloë is good evidence for his contention that the world was planned by an all-wise intelligence and that the complicated machinery of instinctive behavior could not possibly have worked itself out blindly. One may grant, I think, that any explanation of things so improbable will itself sound rather unconvincing. But if one must choose between the two improbabilities, then so preposterous a scheme as that followed by Meloë suggests (to me, at least) millions of years of muddling through rather than intelligent, over-all planning. Could any intelligence not itself deranged have deliberately devised for this terribly handicapped beastling its design for living? That design is preposterous both because it is so inefficiently complex and because the conflict of interests between Meloë and Anthophore is a conflict never adjudicated and never resolved. How can any theist whose God is much more than the sum total of existing forces fail from time to time to fall into the vernacular and to demand of his all-wise Providence: "Look here—whose side are you on, anyway?" A prodigious amount of Schopenhauer's Will must have been expended in elaborating Meloë's scheme of survival. Of Idea there seems to have been precious little.

I am aware that when I permit myself to spend a certain amount of my time watching for the grass to turn green, I am not what most people would consider profitably employed. Probably, moreover, they would think little better of me when I regard with a quizzical eye that Meloë who has happened to cross my path, or when I say to her something like: "Well, well. So you are one of the two out of ten thousand to whom all the unlikely things happened. You won the grand prize in the lottery which has so discouragingly few winning tickets." The philosophical will remind me that the proper study of mankind is man, and the sociologically minded that our political and economic system is at least as fascinatingly inefficient as Meloë's scheme of life, while being, at the same time, of more immediate importance to us.

But I am not so much abashed by such rebukes as some might expect me to be because I am not by any means convinced that there is not some real connection between Meloë's predicament and ours; not convinced that what theologians sometimes call the contingent universe is not so much of a piece as to render the powers which made her what she is something that must be understood before we can understand what makes us what we are and thus, to some extent, limits the possibilities of what we can do about it.

Surely, for example, there is no more fundamental distinction among various philosophies of life, schemes of ethics, and political programs than that which would enable us to put all of them into one of two classes—the class of those which urge us to follow Nature and the class of those which, in some sense, urge us to resist her, to deny that her aims are ours or her methods necessarily those we need to follow. If I lean toward the first, I say to myself that Nature's is not a planned economy or a planned society; that she operates upon the assumption that irreconcilable interests will always exist and that in many instances she allows mere chance to determine how things will turn out. If I lean to the other, I proclaim that the refusal to let Nature take her course is precisely the thing that distinguishes man from the animals and that I will plan my economy and define my logical code of ethics precisely because Nature does no such thing.

Several times I have questioned Meloë on just this point. She has never, I regret to say, deigned to answer me. Like Shelley, who is said to have snatched a baby from its carriage to demand some account of its prenatal existence and its trailing clouds of glory, I have

no recourse but to mutter: "How close they are!" But
I do have the satisfaction of feeling that I have asked
a good question in the right quarter.

Perhaps Meloë does not answer me because she
knows as well as I do that the question, however good
in itself, would only lead to another—if the answer
should be, as I suspect it would, that man need not limit
his projects entirely and absolutely to those which have
already succeeded elsewhere. Just how "unnatural," I
would then want to ask, can we dare to be, and that
question even Meloë probably could not answer if she
would.

Even the most ardent of humanists will have to admit
that in some respects and to some degree we are a part
of a contingent natural universe. Even the most ascetic
of monastic orders make concessions to what the natural body of man requires, and none of them, so far as I
know, advocates subsistence on spiritual nourishment
alone. But if it is all just a question of degree, one must
still wonder whether mankind has made only the first
faint beginnings toward the development of a life separate from Nature or whether, as a persistent protestant
minority continues to suggest, he is already so far gone
in unnatural living that only a realization of that fact
and a return to less artificial ways can save him from
destruction.

Has the machine civilization just begun, or has it
already progressed to the point where it is surely de-

stroying itself? Have we just begun to discover our characteristically human mental life—intellectual, aesthetic, and emotional; have we just begun to discover our true spiritual home among philosophical concepts, mathematical symbols, and abstract art? Or is that mental life already withering because its roots no longer go down into Nature? Is our society just beginning to redeem itself from the anarchy which prevails elsewhere throughout Nature, or is it already so unnatural that it cannot much longer survive? Is it only perverse fancy which suggests the possibility that life itself, in all its forms, is a persistent, self-willed disorder which has disturbed the mathematical orderliness of the nonliving universe and that human society must always be disorderly because men cannot escape the most fundamental of the contingencies determining the kind of Being of which he is a part?

Sixty or seventy miles away from my Connecticut hillside some of these questions are being put to practical and costly test in the city to which I go periodically and from which I return with a sense of peaceful release. During all my summers and nearly half the days of my winter weeks I walk on earth, not asphalt, and see trees, not poles. In many respects I am like—but in some few I hope different from—the usual commuter to whom country week ends are a habit, merely a pleasant change which does not imply any very fundamental break in his external or internal ways of life, and which has no philosophical implications. In so far as I am different; in so far as I am more vividly aware of plant and insect and animal; in so far as I have not to the same extent brought with me the concerns of the city—I am, in the view of many, so much the worse. I have attempted to escape and I have regressed. I am one of those who are rejecting the responsibilities of the present and the future to indulge in nostalgia for an earlier stage of culture now being rapidly left behind.

It may be so. But I have private reasons for being a good deal less than entirely convinced that it is. From where I stand, it rather looks as though Meloë, whom Nature has led to an unusually fantastic predicament, nevertheless may very well have a better chance of survival than Man who has so persistently attempted to take his destiny into his own hands. I do have the inner conviction that when the grass has turned green, something really important has happened and that I might be a good deal less well employed than in taking note of the fact.

Joy, interrupted now and again by pain and terminated ultimately by death, seems the normal course of life in Nature. Anxiety and distress, interrupted occasionally by pleasure, is the normal course of man's existence. Joylessness, the "quiet desperation" which Thoreau defined, may ultimately come to seem the distinctly human characteristic; and in the country I not only escape that to some degree but also participate somewhat in the joy which is not ordinarily ours.

The inner voice has whispered too many different things to too many different men for me to have any conviction that it is always right or that it comes from anywhere except merely from within. But some voices one must listen to, and when this voice speaks to me its authority, however little it may be, is at least as great as the authority of the latest editorial in the latest weekly or monthly review. The hardest facts, as Havelock Ellis once remarked, are the facts of emotion. Joy and love, for example, cannot be doubted when one feels them. I know that they existed *in* me and *for* me when I heard the first peepers of spring and when I watched spring turn to summer. I cannot regret that I did so. I hope that whether the rest of the world is headed toward success or failure in its largest enterprises, I shall be permitted to watch with equal satisfaction at least one spring come again.

June

Spring Rain

One trouble with the city is that there is so much bad weather there. Nearly everybody admits that snow is merely an expensive nuisance, and even the early summer rains serve no real purpose where there is nothing to be watered and where sewers have to be built to drain the insipid liquid away. Some day, no doubt, when we have become thoroughly urbanized, whole areas will be roofed over and the ideal amount of ultraviolet supplied by electricity. Children can be taken occasionally to the country to see what the sun looks like as they are taken now to see a hill or a mountain. Probably many of them will not want to go anyway, for the country will be to them only what it was to the London club man: "A damp sort of place where all sorts of birds fly about uncooked." But that will be all right too—for those who like it.

The good thing about the country is, on the other hand, that we don't have there any bad weather at all—only a number of different kinds of good. In fact I should be willing to maintain that there, and there only, do we have what has any right to be called weather at all—as distinguished, I mean, from those mere inclemencies of one kind or another, which do no more than make the difference between a day when it is convenient to walk to the subway and one when the only choice is between getting messy and uncomfortable trying to walk, and getting equally messy and uncomfortable waiting for the taxi which, of course, some luckier people have already taken.

Sometimes, I will admit, even in the country we do have rather too much of one kind of good weather for too long at a time—as we have been having it just now when rain has been falling and falling and falling as though some sorcerer's apprentice had forgotten how to turn it off. Even the thirstiest flowers do not need that much water; they are in danger of being drowned out. And the situation inclines one to the suspicion that Nature is not, as some philosophers have insisted, a Golden Mean, but essentially intemperate, never knowing when to stop, whether it is in pouring down raindrops or multiplying seed. At least the living things

seem to go on getting bigger and more numerous and
more extravagant until something not themselves puts
a stop to it.

I have never lived long enough in England to get the
real English point of view which expresses itself when
the countryman looks out of the window at the steady
sleety drizzle and says—as I have heard him say in all
seriousness—"What a lovely day for a walk!" I do go
out in the rain from time to time but not for long, and
I conclude somewhat pusillanimously that this kind of
good weather is enjoyed best when looked at through a
window rather than when actually participated in.

Thank goodness I do not feel any obligation to do
what some people call "catching up with their reading"
—which means, generally, reading the things they don't
want to read but do at least skim through, because
someone is going to ask them about the latest novel, or
even perhaps discover that the *Odyssey* is for them,
literally, a closed book. But notoriously a rainy day is
a good time to read and I do read a little bit of everything, including the works of those who have tried before me to get down on paper a hint of what the privilege of living with some awareness of other living things
has meant to them.

A learned scholar has discovered several score of different, distinguishable meanings of the word "Nature"
as used in the eighteenth century alone. No wonder,

then, that people do not always agree when they are
using the same term to indicate so many different things.
But none of the disagreements has ever struck me more
forcibly than one which seems to rise independently of
this rather elementary semantic difficulty, though it no
doubt involves other more elusive ones. I mean the
disagreement over the question whether Nature is
"cruel" or "kind."

Not only individuals but whole ages or periods have
tended to disagree with one another and to make alter-
nately the most sweepingly irreconcilable generalizations. Dryden, speaking for the children of Thomas
Hobbes, was almost post-Darwinian (or Herbert Spen-
cerian) when he proclaimed that "Self-Defence is
Nature's eldest law." Burns, roughly a century later,
talks about "Nature's social union" as something which
only heartless man disturbs; and before long Words-
worth had got around to believing that "Nature never
did betray the heart that loved her." Then, a generation later, Tennyson was back to Dryden and beyond
with his "red in tooth and claw." One begins to suspect
that there must be something wrong with a question
that can be answered in so many different ways.

Perhaps Nature cannot very well be a thing that does
not exist except in the human mind. "Kindness" and
"cruelty" imply intention or, at the very least, awareness of being the one or the other. But does either intention or that kind of awareness exist except in us? I

have often wondered and I am by no means sure. There is hardly a stroll in the woods, hardly a glance out of the window, which does not raise the question. Is the weasel in the chicken house, notoriously given to wanton killing, aware of cruelty; and is the solicitous mother-fox aware of kindness? Are they more like the earthquake and the spring sun than like the human tyrant and the fond human parent? Not quite like either is my guess, but somewhere in between. Perhaps, even, they are just what some human beings seem willing to accept as ideal for themselves and the scientific society of the future. Perhaps they are what sometimes gets praised these days as "unsentimental," "realistic," and "objective."

One of my cats used to roll on snakes. She would find a specimen of convenient size—say, about eighteen inches long—carry it onto the lawn, and then treat it like a bed of catnip. A neighbor, more imaginative than I, watched the performance one day and concluded, since the snake made no effort to get away, that he liked it too. I am sufficiently cautious not to go on record as agreeing, but at least the snake seemed to be suffering no great discomfort and might, when the cat tired, slip away into a stone wall with an experience to tell the children about. Many a legend in the vast oral literature of unnatural history has been based on less. Cats love snakes and snakes love cats; they go on petting parties together.

That particular cat has gone the way of her kind (and of ours) but she left a son whose interest in reptiles expresses itself in less kindly fashion. I have seen him with a feline companion sitting gravely in front of a good-sized garter snake which from time to time would rear. When it did so, the cats took turns at reaching out a long, cautious paw and giving a quick firm tap, just on the top of the snake's head. The snake would subside, and the two would then sit quietly until there was an opportunity to repeat the performance. How long that would have gone on or how it would have ended if I had not intervened, I do not know.

"How like a cat!" the ailurophobe will exclaim. "How essentially cruel, even though in this case it was only mildly so!" But a cat will wait in exactly the same way for a leaf to blow, and perhaps the greatest difference between him and us is not that he is crueler than we nor even that he is less intelligent, but simply that he lacks our power to project ourselves into another's situation; to see anything from any point of view except his own; to understand, in a word, that anything except himself (and, dimly, the friend who feeds him) is alive. Neither the snake nor the leaf is "me," and neither, therefore, can be said to count. Perhaps the ability to do just this thing that the cat cannot do—namely, project himself—is one of the most significant as well as one of the most troubling of man's distinguishing characteristics; and perhaps, incidentally, it is the characteristic which an attempt to live with some awareness of Nature as a whole seeks to exploit.

On another occasion I saw the same two cats when they had ganged-up on a young squirrel to whom, so far, no harm had been done. All three were perfectly still; the two cats were so placed that the unfortunate victim could not possibly escape, and all three were waiting—the one in terror, the others calmly aware of their advantage. Movie-goers have seen precisely that scene in underworld pictures: The two thugs in the closed room stare quietly at the helpless heroine; they do not do anything, they do not need to do anything at the moment; they can wait. But there is no move that the heroine can make. If she runs or if she screams, then the sinister silence will give way to the brutal act. The moments stretch out. It will not be the thugs whose patience will be exhausted. But how long can the fatal moment be put off? How long, indeed, is it worth while to put off what must happen sooner or later? "You," say the cold eyes of the gangsters, "say when." In the picture, of course, the improbable rescuer always arrives in the nick of time. In Nature, unfortunately, he often does not.

W. H. Hudson made it a rule not to intervene in any of Nature's dramas. He never intentionally harmed a wild creature, but neither did he ever attempt to help one. Long experience had convinced him that the attempt to play God did not work—at least when one wasn't God and therefore lacked the omniscience and the omnipotence necessary to straighten out this scheme of things which may or may not be a sorry scheme but which in any case very complicatedly *is*. I do not always follow Hudson's rule, and I intervened this time to save the heroine-squirrel from the gangster-cats, as I have often done before. She did get away, but I am rather more inclined to believe that the cats were resentful and hurt than that she was grateful. At least they looked resentful, and she did not look as though she had understood that my intentions were good—or even that I had had any. Moreover, I am sure that if the cats were indignant, they felt it as a righteous indignation. It was rather I than they who had been guilty of pure malice. I had taken away something they wanted.

As for me, I felt mildly virtuous; convinced, indeed, that if I had been consulted in the ordering of the universe, I would have seen to it that things like this would not be so typical a part of it as they are. But I was not sure that I had accomplished so very much. I could not follow the squirrel around indefinitely. Next day, or the day after that, she may very well have suffered an end no more pleasant—and I always feel the same way after I have violated Hudson's rule.

When I was younger, I once undertook to teach rather sternly still another cat not to catch the birds which he had been proudly bringing to me in the house. At last I seemed to have succeeded. A week, two weeks, finally a month, went by, during which no feathered corpses were seen. I was sure I had succeeded. Then one day I noticed a few feathers in the long eyebrows above the calm, candid eyes. Obviously my cat had no sense of guilt. He had managed to grasp the fact that for some obscure human reason, not worth trying to understand, I did not want dead birds in the house, but that even I should suppose that catching a bird could be, in itself, something to be ashamed of rather than proud of was so absurd as never to be considered.

I accepted the situation. Men and cats can get along together very well—as well, indeed, as people with irreconcilable political or religious differences, but under the same conditions: namely, that the differences remain undiscussed and, above all, that neither tries to change the other.

A visiting acquaintance remained indignant and would not admit the parallel when I reminded him that he himself had just dined heartily off roast chicken, and that I could not see how it made much difference if I had thoughtfully arranged for someone else to do the bloody work for him. "That cat," he said, "is well-fed at home." "You," I replied, "could eat beans." And until I am willing myself to give up meat, I am not going to feel morally superior to cats, on this score at least.

Here then is another aspect of the fact that this universe of ours is contingent. William Cowper, the most morbidly gentle of men, wrote a poem to a spaniel who chased after birds—and then, in a spirit of laudable fair-mindedness, he wrote the spaniel's reply:

> Sir! when I flew to seize the bird,
>   In spite of your command,
> A louder voice than yours I heard,
>   And harder to withstand:
>
> You cried—Forbear!—but in my breast
>   A mightier cried—Proceed!
> 'Twas nature, Sir, whose strong behest
>   Impell'd me to the deed.
>
> .   .   .   .   .
>
> If killing birds be such a crime,
>   (Which I can hardly see)
> What think you, Sir, of killing Time
>   With verse address'd to me?

Meanwhile we do the best we can, testing the contingencies here and there, assuring ourselves that certain of them really are ineluctable; even, perhaps, rebelling and protesting a little when we think we have discovered that they actually are. At least my squirrel got away that time. Perhaps she was lucky the day after; perhaps saved again by something else the day after that. And if she finally came to an end, good or bad, so does everyone else. I had put the end off for one more day and that is all anyone can do, for himself or for anyone. My dentist, patching up a tooth, warned me that I must understand, of course, that this was only temporary, and he seemed startled when I replied that so, after all, was life itself. What should so temporary a creature as I want with a really permanent set of teeth? They might possibly be of interest to some future anthropologist, but I can have no need for them.

Perhaps some real, faintly conscious cruelty is possible among the "higher" animals. At least I am evolutionist enough to suppose that since man is capable of it then it must have a rudimentary beginning below his level. But certainly it plays no very large part in animal life; is not, as it can become for some men, a principal aim. It is no part of Nature's "simple plan," however many cruel things may happen incidentally or be the result of aims ruthlessly pursued. The aboriginal will to live, the urge which long ago persuaded the chemical compound to become an enzyme, the enzyme to become a bacterium, and, finally, the anthropoid to become a man, was neither kindly nor cruel, but an urge and no more. It did not want to live in love or to live in hate, but simply to live; and Nature, as a whole, is still, more fundamentally than she is anything else, that urge.

Often enough—and often justifiably—your ordinary lover of Nature has been accused of sentimentality. He prattles, so his condemners say, of the sweet twitter of birds and of the flowers that bloom in the spring. He disregards the seamy side of things and sees the world in greeting-card terms. The cute kitten and the Easter bunny are his symbols. He never asks of the tiger: "Did He who made the lamb make thee?" But since about the middle of the nineteenth century another kind of sentimentality has been at least as prevalent and a good deal more respectable—what might be called, I mean, the sentimentality of violence. If to feel a false emotion based upon a deliberately incomplete view of the facts is to be guilty of sentimentalism, then the view that Nature is consistently violent and cruel is as sentimental as its opposite. She is no more characteristically red in tooth and claw than she is characteristically a kind mother. She is both, or neither, or something that includes and transcends the two. What is commonly called the realistic view is as sentimental as what is commonly called sentimental.

No doubt it is human to insist upon the adequacy of a simple "either or." No doubt it is not only human, but laudably so, to distinguish throughout the animal—even throughout the vegetable and inanimate—world between what, in us, would be kindliness on the one hand and cruelty on the other. Even a storm we call "fierce," and a spring sun "caressing." If Nature is neutral, we are not. The ability to set up dichotomies is one of the most fateful of the abilities that man has

June

discovered in himself. But though we cannot and should not live permanently in what may or may not actually be the valueless world Nature sometimes appears, it is nevertheless our privilege to enjoy the dizzy pleasure of occasional moments when we seem almost to have left humanity behind and to survey the world—from some high, more than Himalayan peak—*sub specie aeternitatis.*

This rain, for instance, which has been falling, falling, falling. If it interferes with our plans we call it "hateful," but that is only a turn of speech and few people are naïve enough really to suppose that the rain actually intended to spoil the picnic they had planned. Some few more—but no longer, I suppose, very many—are capable of believing that it comes in answer to some farmer's prayer, or, if it lasts too long, as punishment for some sin of the community. Yet we are no more than one step removed from so simple a philosophy when we assume in a more general way that Nature's intentions are somehow benevolent or the opposite; that she "means" well or ill for us or her other children. Their needs and their desires are too various for her to be able to favor them all. She could not, even if she would, be good to each and every one. She is cruel to the rabbit put into the mouth of a fox but kind to the fox's cubs to whom she has given a dinner. The child who wept over the picture of the Christian martyrs in the arena because she was so sorry for "that poor lion over there who hasn't got any Christian" was a true philosopher.

"There was never yet," of course, "philosopher that could endure the toothache patiently." If this spring rain were a hurricane, even if the water should get too seriously into my basement, I should soon enough begin to lose my serenity and to see the thing *sub specie temporis.* So far, however, the basement is dry and there is no immediate prospect that the price of vegetables will rise still further as the result of too wet a season. I am still, therefore, a philosopher. The rain, I can still say a bit smugly, falleth upon the just and the unjust. It has no intentions. It is good for those who can take some advantage of it; bad for those whom it will drown or rot. "The stars are little twinkling rogues who light us home sometimes when we are drunk but care for neither you nor me nor any man." I can, in other words, if not accept the universe, then at least accept that small part of it which is calling my attention to itself at the moment.

July

A Mere Matter of Size

Do pitchmen on street corners and at country fairs still sell, as in my youth they did, little one-lens microscopes in a shiny brass tube? At one end was an ordinary, low-powered magnifier which was removed for use. At the other was a tiny block of glass, convex on one surface and flat on the opposite one. The pitchman was usually provided with some pond water, or perhaps a bit of overripe cheese, and before inviting the spectator to take a look he would put a smear of the one or the other on the plane surface. Many were unable to resist the appeal of the marvel and carried one of the instruments home—in some cases, perhaps, starting a child on the road that might lead ultimately to a laboratory and a biologist's career.

The principle of the thing was precisely the same as that of the celluloid paper-cutters brought back from Niagara Falls and offering the spectator who peeped through the tiny bit of glass, set in the handle, an astonishingly enlarged view either of the Falls, or (if the owner was a wag) of some pathetically decorous dancer in cautiously abbreviated costume. As a matter of fact, moreover, these "novelties," far from being new, were of very honorable lineage and had come down in the world. In their use of one very small lens they were the same as those which Anton van Leeuwenhoek had employed when, for the first time in history, a bacterium was seen by a human eye. His instruments were far better than the earliest compound microscopes, and those sold at country fairs were better still because they embodied a much later optician's ingenious idea of putting the object to be examined on one surface of the lens itself. This avoids the complexities introduced when light travels through one glass into the air and back into glass again, and it helps to make the definition very good indeed.

But why did this particular marvel make the appeal it obviously did to the yokels of both town and country? As I remember it, the pitchman's spiel included, for the benefit of the merely practical, the suggestion that the unwary were continually eating bugs of various kinds and that what he was offering them for a quarter could be used to peer at one's food in order to make sure that it was not crawling with loathsome or dangerous creatures. So far as this was taken seriously, it no doubt contributed to an increase in the number of neurotics and cranks; but I do not think that most of the purchasers had as their chief motive a determination to protect themselves against contaminated food.

What the little microscope did do was to stir in the memory of the spectator his dim awareness of certain persistent human fancies connected with the ancient concept of the microcosm and the macrocosm. Those fancies are, of course, far older than the microscope itself and quite possibly arise spontaneously in minds which have never met the historical doctrine. What it meant originally was that man was a little universe and that the universe was a kind of organism. Perhaps there is no logical connection between that assumption and the belief that there is a little invisible world that repeats every feature of the great visible one. But the connection seems to have been made as far back as the earliest microscopists, who long persisted in seeing analogies between protozoic and human anatomy. "Great fleas have little fleas to bite 'em" is one of the things which strike the imagination as inherently probable, and what the yokel saw was not so much something new as a confirmation of what he had always half-consciously believed. "The unseen" does not mean merely the immaterial. It means also the things that are too small or too big to be seen by human eyes.

July

As a boy I graduated from the pitchmen's little gadgets to a cheap compound microscope and, finally, to a really good if old-fashioned instrument, lent me by a doctor. As a young man I bought a fine researcher's outfit, far better than I had any need for, and occasionally I use it still, feeling very important as I manipulate its rather complicated adjustments and finally see a paramecium or, possibly, the beautifully named and beautifully shaped *Lacrimaria* swim into view. As a matter of fact this is normally a part of those rites of spring which I religiously perform year after year.

The rites always include the inspection of a marsh from which the ice is just disappearing, in order to see if the painted and the spotted turtles are yet stirring and if the salamanders have yet laid the glutenous masses of eggs which mysteriously appear a good bit before those of the earliest frogs. It also ordinarily includes carrying home in a jar a sample of the water. Every year life begins again in the ponds as, presumably, it began there in the springtime of creation when the dry land was still lifeless.

Most of your microscopic, one-celled animals lie low in the winter like their larger and more complicated fellow creatures. Reduced then to something very like a seed, or, even more closely, like a grain of pollen, they have been resting motionless in the mud until the season was ready to call them forth again. Few things will be stirring before they do and that is all part of Nature's far from simple plan. For though the protozoan is not the very first in the series of the things which eat and then are eaten, he is very nearly that. There must be bacteria about for him to consume, but he comes next after them. Many slightly larger creatures cannot flourish until he is abundant, and they, in turn, are necessary for those somewhat larger than themselves. Each spring the system must get started again from the beginning with everything appearing in its proper order. And somehow it always does.

Hunting protozoa in spring is like hunting anything else at that season. It is the fact that one finds relatively so little which makes it exciting when one finds anything at all, and if it's multitude and variety that one seeks, one must choose a different season. That is why I usually carry my bottle to the pond again in May or June or, as this year, even later, when the microscopic fauna and flora are at the height of their flourishing. In midsummer the numbers will decline again, but now the water is swarming. Pick up one drop of it and you can hardly miss something strange and wonderful.

A biologist who made a census at the end of April found in a New England lake an average of thirty protozoa alone per cubic centimeter of water. But that counts only one particular class of animal. Occupying the same cubic centimeter, there are almost certain to be microscopic plants—possibly one or more of the brilliantly green and gracefully shaped desmids, even more probably one to a score or more of the sculptured, glass-enclosed diatoms with incised designs so delicate that microscopists use them to test the perfection of their lenses. Besides that, there may well be rotifers and possibly, just large enough to be seen easily by the naked eye, a green hydra with its devil-fish tentacles ready to grasp a tiny crustacean unlucky enough to pass by. Finally, for the really fortunate there may be—especially if the cubic centimeter includes a fragment from a water-lily pad—some specimens of *Floscularia ringens,* enclosed in tubes of translucent tortoise-shell beads from which protrudes the rhythmically waving crown of tiny hairs so perfectly creating the illusion of circular motion that it is no wonder the organism was named by the early microscopists Rotifer, or Wheel Animalcule.

Animal lovers unwilling to deny animals any of even the dubious privileges sometimes assumed for human beings have occasionally been troubled by the question whether or not there could be room in heaven for the souls of everything that once lived. And unless one is ready to believe with Descartes that the soul is located in the pituitary gland and that only man has one, where shall we stop? If the hunter goes, accompanied by his dog, then what shall exclude the rabbit he chased? And if you admit the rabbit, why not everything on down the line to the rotifer and the paramecium? Nor, to tell the truth, do I see where there is any difficulty even on the unlikely assumption that souls take up room. If there is space and to spare for twenty-five living protozoa in one cubic centimeter of water, then perhaps there is space and to spare for all that ever lived in the universe which has offered to the eye of the camera nebulae floating millions—or is it billions?—of light-years away. Even if the soul of a rotifer takes up space, it does not seem likely that it can take up very much. Perhaps the very first to be created are now occupying some heaven of their own on some planet circling around one of the suns whose countless numbers constitute the faint milky glow of the great nebula in Andromeda.

A woman friend who once consented to peer down the tube of my microscope presently took her eye away and asked, with an air of wild surmise: "Are they real?" My impulse was, of course, to laugh. But the question had behind it something more elusive than at first may appear and was not quite so foolish as it sounded. She did not mean, "Do they have material existence?" It would not have answered her question if I had replied that of course they do, and that as a matter of fact they are astonishingly like, almost embarrassingly like, both one of the individual cells of our bodies and those bodies as a whole. They are single cells of protoplasm, but also single cells which can do many more different things than any one kind of our own can do. Neither would it have done any good to tell her that a generation ago it became possible, through the rigging up of a very ingenious device, actually to dissect one of these invisible creatures and that the little expanding and contracting spot which she could see in a paramecium was actually, in all-too-human fashion, excreting uric acid in quantities sufficient to be detected by the microchemist.

No, the question she was asking was not one which things like this could answer. She had no vocabulary to use in formulating the conception she was really struggling with, and it was perhaps a metaphysical one. What she really meant was: "What does it mean to say that I can see what I cannot see, that these creatures exist for me only when peered at through this totally mysterious instrument, and that they simply aren't there when I look directly at the slide with the drop of water on it? Is what is real only when seen under very special conditions really real? Obviously this microcosm is real to itself and in its own terms. But is its universe continuous with mine? Can I reach it in any other way? Does it exist for me except during the few moments when I am peering down the tube?"

Perhaps she was even dimly alarmed by the half-formulated question whether or not the acceptance of the microcosm as "real" means an obligation to expand still further the limits of that fellowship of living creatures which man has tended more and more to acknowledge. We, or at least many of us, no longer treat horses and dogs and cats ruthlessly. We accept to some extent their right to live and to escape unnecessary suffering. But where does our fellowship and our responsibility draw the line? Most would probably agree that the refusal, recommended by the poet, to step wantonly upon even a worm is carrying things pretty far. "We are all in this together"; does that include the paramecium too? But if, to use Donne's now almost too familiar metaphor, a man is not an island but part of a continent, and if (to go one step farther) that continent is the continent, not merely of mankind, but of all living things; if, in a word, we feel even now an impulse to rescue a squirrel from a cat, shall we also come in time to turn away in horror when the hydra clasps a water flea? If not, then at what point do we call a halt? Am I being "sentimental" when I rescue the squirrel, or am I being "brutal" when I step on the caterpillar?

With some embarrassment I confess that I have pondered this question as well as the even more elusive implications of my friend's inquiry. For those more elusive questions, too, are interesting. My relation to the protozoa is curiously like my relation to the men in Mars—or like what it will be when and if we establish television communication with them. The protozoa also are known to us only through the intermediary of an instrument. That is the only way we shall ever know them. We cannot get down into their world any more than we could get up into the world of the Martians. In fact they are, theoretically, even less accessible; for though even now men speculate about the problems that would be involved in interplanetary rocket-travel and about the question whether or not they are solvable, no one can even begin to imagine a method for getting into a drop of water. Utter disparity of size interposes a barrier, sets up a discontinuity, more unbridgeable than a vast stretch of space. As a matter of fact, what I see through my microscope strikes me as considerably more strange than the Martians whom I may some day see on the television screen. The question "Are they real?" is rather less foolish as applied to micro-organisms than it would be to the electronic image of a Martian.

Some years ago the *New Yorker* magazine published a drawing of a group of scientists around a microscope. The one who has been doing the looking has just turned away in alarm and is saying to his companions: "Gentlemen, we had better leave quietly. I think they have noticed us." The situation would not have struck readers as comic if they had not been at least dimly aware that its premise ignores the existence of a discontinuity which they had always taken for granted. And there are many instances that might be used to show that it poses one of those questions which are capable of fascinating almost any human mind once it is grasped.

Nothing else can, for example, explain the renown of Fitz James O'Brien's short story "The Diamond Lens," of which anthologists are so fond. It is not really a very good story. The invention is feeble, the pseudo-scientific apparatus childishly unconvincing and ignorant. But the simple, central conception, that of a man who becomes enamored of an ultramicroscopic girl, reduces everything to the simplest possible terms. What love could possibly be more hopeless, what love object more completely inaccessible? Mr. Will Cuppy plays even more lightly with the same idea when, in one of his strange books of more or less natural history, he gives directions for raising protozoa in a goldfish bowl and remarks that, once you have got used to it, you will not mind not being able to see your pets.

It is not, mind you, that these creatures are much unlike us, except in size, for their strangeness is not a matter of difference but merely of the discontinuity which a great disparity of magnitude establishes. Like us they are composed of protoplasm, and this implies the very closest and most essential kinship that can exist between two things. Any of the cells which compose our own bodies would recognize them, though they might marvel at the versatility of the protozoan which can not only react kinetically but also digest and secrete and reproduce independent of the assistance of any other cell.

William Congreve, long before the theory of evolution had suggested that all animals are genetically related, once remarked that he could never pass a cage of monkeys without a certain embarrassment. There are moments when I have been capable of feeling at the microscope the same emotion, since these remote creatures do nevertheless demonstrate in many of their actions their right to be considered brothers. Their love affairs are carried to a singularly complete conclusion, for in "conjunction," as the biologists call it, the two cells fuse completely and the two lovers become one, thus actually realizing an ideal which it has long been the habit of human lovers to profess to desire. And I have often wondered if Jacques Loeb's discovery that a perfect epidemic of conjunction could be produced in a protozoan culture by the simple process of reducing the available food to the starvation level really gives the key to the understanding of a certain human phenomenon.

It has often been observed that young people who are penniless and without prospects often show a strong tendency to marry. Is it possible that the explanation is not on the psychological level, where one would be inclined to seek it, but rather on the protoplasmic? Is it possible that two people who find existence very precarious tend to pool their lack of resources because the protoplasm which they share with the protozoa impels them to do so? I am not prepared to work out the theory but I give the hint freely to any sociologist who can use it.

Once late at night I had the privilege of discussing with a very famous astronomer Einstein's theory that the universe is finite rather than infinite. He said that he rather thought it was, though this did not mean that there might not be more than one finite universe. "Might there," I asked, "be an infinite number of finite universes?" "Yes," he said; "although," he added hastily, "you understand that they would all be absolutely discontinuous." "And what," I asked, "is the nature of that discontinuity?"

The famous astronomer looked at his watch. "Good gracious, I've got to catch a train—er—will you repeat that question?" I did so. "Well," he said, "it's not spatial, and it's not temporal. It's——I *do* have to go." Thirty seconds later, the door through which he had gone out opened again to admit his head. "If I ever find out about the nature of that discontinuity, I'll let you know."

I have never heard from him since, and I suppose that he never has found out. But to me the idea of that completely ungraspable discontinuity is rather less interesting than the less elusive but still sufficiently puzzling discontinuity between me and my microscopic fellows. It is an ancient platitude to say that to peer through a telescope into the immensities of space makes a human being feel very small. One might think, therefore, that peering through a microscope would make him feel very great. But it doesn't. This also makes him feel small, humbled in the face of the incomprehensibly little. For what the two experiences have in common is more important than the contrast between them. In both cases, we are brought face to face with the sense of a discontinuity, the sense of being eternally shut off from something which is, nevertheless, as real (and perhaps as important) as we are. The world is so full of a number of things. And we are only one of them.

This summer I have been looking again at Paramecia and Lacrimaria and Opalina, as well as at the flora amidst which they live. But I do not know what kind of relation I have with them or just how I feel toward them. I marvel and I admire. They are beautiful. They are, quite literally, lovely. But in what sense do or can I love them? After I have peered for a while at a drop of water, I wipe it off with a piece of tissue and put it into a wastebasket. I should not be telling the truth if I said that I feel much compunction at such wanton killing. Why don't I? Is it simply because responsibility cannot bridge the gap of that discontinuity established by nothing but size? Do I, like my woman friend, doubt that the protozoa are real?

August

The Dead of Summer

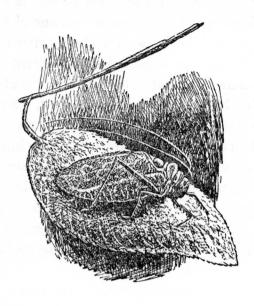

This is the very dead of summer. I am not sure that I ever heard just that phrase before, but I don't see why not. Surely, it describes at least the impression that August creates as she slumbers, replete and satisfied. Spring was a fever and autumn will be a regret, but this is the month too aware of its own successful achievement to be more than barely sentient. The growth which continues seems without effort, like the accumulation of fat. If Nature is ever purely *vegetative,* it is now. She is but barely conscious.

The season of seed and fruit lies just ahead, but it is already assured and inevitable. The epoch of competition and doubt is past, the weeks when the individual did not know whether or not he was one of those who would get along in the world. The survivors are complacent; the coming months of retrenchment and death are too far away to cast a shadow, and it is at this time if ever that Nature is bourgeois. At least, August is the month when the solid and the domestic triumph, when the prudent come into their own. The very birds, whose springtime was devoted to love and music, are now responsible parents who have forgotten how to sing. The early flowers of the woods waved their brief blossoms and are forgotten, but the roadsides and the fields are taken over now by the strong, coarse, and confident weeds.

If the bold premature piping of the frog symbolizes spring, and the plaintive, never-say-die stridulation of the cricket symbolizes autumn, then, to me, the woodchuck embodies the spirit of summer. I see him, fat and sleek, pushing his way through the tall grass down the bank which leads to my old apple tree. From time to time he rears to peer about for danger, but by now this is hardly more than a habit—he is not really afraid. He picks up an apple or pretends that one weed is more succulent than another. Presently he will waddle away again, confident that he has been laying up, in his very belly, treasures that moths will not corrupt and no thief break through to steal.

So far as the plant kingdom is concerned, this is the

epoch of the Compositae, those efficient producers of
seed which represent Nature's latest, most improved
model. Their teeming co-operative flower heads have
reduced the wasteful display of petal to the minimum
and some of them have learned to dispense with it entirely, like a society which has got rid of the frills. Unmistakably they are inheriting the earth. "Give us a few
more million years," they seem to be saying, "and we
will show you how the world ought really to be run.
Produce, distribute and consume. It is only a problem
of technology, of chemistry, and of mechanism."

Perhaps it is unfortunate that this is the time which
your ordinary city dweller is most likely to choose for
his brief annual visit to the country. No doubt it is the
season when the town is most uncomfortable, and he
thinks more of what he is getting away from than of
what he is coming to. But there is no other period when
Nature is so little dramatic. Even the countryman himself will tend to fall, if he does not watch himself, into
Nature's own mood of somnolent content. He loses
something of his alertness now that he is neither startled
by newness, nor reminded (as soon he will be) that
summer, which seems so motionlessly established, will
not last forever. He can hardly believe that there was a
spring or that there will ever be a winter.

Moreover, and what is even worse, he may find himself becoming a bit bourgeois himself, a little inclined
to take too complacently for granted the warmth and

flourishing abundance, to ask fewer questions, to be aware of fewer ecstasies as well as fewer doubts. He is less a pilgrim and more of a land-owner. He looks about at "my house" and "my woods" and "my fields." He thinks of owning things and covets his neighbor's land. He wonders if the proprietor of that strip across the road might be persuaded to sell.

This question of ownership, of property, is a thorny one. Thoreau thought he had solved it when he concluded that he had taken possession of whatever he had enjoyed and that, recorded deeds notwithstanding, the fields he wandered over belonged more truly to him than to the nominal proprietor who had no idea what was going on in them. But for most people, at least, it is not quite so simple. "Mine" is a warm and colorful word which it is possible to utter with many intonations and with many intentions. It may mean "keep off." It may also mean what it means when we say "my home" or "my brother." August is the month to ponder it without too much disfavor. It is the time when the plant has established its right to a few square inches of soil, the bird to its nesting site and the woodchuck to his burrow.

There are some to whom the neighbor's fields always look greener; that is acquisitiveness and envy. There are others to whom it is their own things that seem the best—even though only their own catbird or their own tall spire of purple wild lettuce. And that is something not objectionable in August or in any other month. There is, for example, a certain tree-frog which I own; who is "mine." He is a *Hyla versicolor*—a larger first cousin of the spring peeper—and he has spent many hours of five successive summers sitting on the edge of a decayed knothole in an apple tree a few feet from the front door. Obviously that knothole is "his." I have taken a great deal of pleasure in having this tree-frog for mine and I am sorry to have to say that apparently he does not reciprocate.

Several times, out of a sheer selfish desire to make him acknowledge that, from a frog's point of view, I am good for something, I have elevated some tidbit, on the end of a straw, under his very nose. Twice he has snatched it casually; twice, when I became very insistent, he impatiently brushed it away with his foreleg. But usually he simply stares motionless and straight ahead after the fashion of the Buddha he so much resembles. Frogs, he tells me, do not need men. They can get along very well without them, would rather not acknowledge their existence. The sense of independence is worth more than an occasional supererogatory worm. Mankind, so far as frogs are concerned, serves no useful purpose. There is no teleological explanation for the human race's existence.

I have also done something else which he would never do for me or for anyone. I wrote to a great expert

on the Amphibia to ask a question that none of my
books ever even raised. Do tree-frogs commonly return,
year after year, to the same station? They are said to
make an annual journey to the pond for love and repro-
duction. Has "my" frog forgotten this call of pleasure
and duty? Is he old, or is he prematurely philosophical?
Or does the fact that I have noticed his absence during
a period between his first appearance and early summer
mean that he woke from a winter sleep in the hole,
made his pilgrimage to the water, and then, on five successive occasions, returned across the woods and fields
to "his" home?

The great authority took the trouble to answer me
courteously and at considerable length. He offered a
number of facts about frogs in general and tree-frogs
in particular. But, so far as my specific questions were
concerned, it all boiled down to "I don't know." "I don't
know what your own particular frog has done and I
don't know what the species in general does." He suggested, of course, what had already occurred to me—
namely, the possibility (at least) that it wasn't actually the same individual year after year. But the appearance is too regular, the particular hole too like many
others which are not inhabited and never to my knowledge have been. He even suggested that there was a
rather awkward way of banding frogs for identification,
as birds are banded. But I do not think I shall try the
experiment. I think I know my frog. Besides, if one had

two friends who could be told apart only by banding, would one really care which of them one was talking to?

I shall not try to pretend that I own nothing except in the sense that I own my frog and that Thoreau thought he owned the best part of his neighbors' fields. I am not so pure as all that. But I should like to think that most of my feeling of proprietorship is at least tinged and softened by some admixture of this more admirable kind of possessiveness. For certainly there are two kinds of owning. One of them has to do with the power complex. Its very essence is the ability and the right to control, to change, and to destroy; most of all, perhaps, to destroy. "Gee up, all my fine horses," said Little Klaus to the mixed team of his own and his neighbor's beasts. Then Big Klaus, because his sense of one kind of ownership was outraged, killed those which were not legally his just to prove that, in actual fact, he owned them all.

That story from Hans Christian Andersen is the very first story I remember having heard, and perhaps it made an impression so deep because it so perfectly typifies—better even than the story of the dog in the manger—the meaning of one kind of ownership. Also, perhaps, because it suggests by contrast the other kind; the kind whose essence is intimacy and responsibility, the privilege of communication and understanding. Both kinds are in Nature. The bird has "his" territory and also "his" fledglings. No wonder, then, that both kinds are in human nature too. But human beings differ more from one another than do the individuals composing any other species of animal. And you can observe that difference in their attitudes toward what they own, especially in the cases where the thing owned is capable of inspiring either of the two emotions.

I do not suppose that there is more than one way of owning a bond, a block of stock, or a trust fund held in perpetuity—comforting though the last must be. But decidedly there are at least two ways of owning a house, a farm, a dog, or even a child. Everyone has observed the difference among his own acquaintances in their attitudes toward the house where they live, and, if they are lucky, the land which may be theirs to go with it. Probably most of us know some father or mother who "has" a son or daughter almost in the fashion that Big Klaus "had" his horses. But it is in the ownership of animals that the difference most clearly appears. It is not a question of how much they are valued, or how large a part they play in the thoughts of their owners, but entirely a question of *why* they are valued and *why* they are thought about.

I remember that I was once in a company which included an important financier and collector of modern art who also "had," as a matter of course, a very fine country estate complete with dogs, horses, and prize poultry. I was chatting, not with him but with my neighbor on the other side, about pets, and for the want of anything better to say, remarked—quite untruthfully —that what I should really like to have was a hippopotamus. The financier heard this remark through one ear and he was alarmed—largely, I suspect, because I had a connection with one of his casual enterprises and he was afraid that I was insane. He turned suddenly towards me to demand: "Why on earth would you want a hippopotamus?" And I was inspired to make an answer which I thought would allay his fears. "Why, don't you see?" I said. "A hippopotamus would be the most expensive pet one could possibly have. The cost of keeping him would be enormous. I could say to myself: 'If I can have a hippopotamus, I could have any pet I could possibly want.'" Relief and comprehension took immediate possession of his countenance. "I see," he said, and turned back to his own companion. But he had revealed very clearly why he owned dogs and horses as well as some very costly examples of modern painting.

I am afraid that a great many people who boast of being, and in fact believe themselves to be, horse-lovers and dog-lovers actually love them no more than my fancier loved his prize poultry or loves the hippopotamus which, for all I know, he may before now have bought just in order to show that he could actually have what I spoke of as an impossibility. Gérard de Nerval presumably did not really love the lobster he is said to have led about Paris on a ribbon to attract attention.

August

I see no reason to suppose that some of the most passionate horse and dog fanciers who own, breed, and travel about from show to show love their prize-winners any more. The fact that a man is proud of his winning boxers no more proves that he loves dogs than the equally proud wearer of a mink coat demonstrates thereby her love of minks—which is not generally supposed to be the reason for wearing their skins. Professed cat-lovers are a good deal less numerous than professed lovers of dogs, and I suspect that there is a sound reason for their tendency to consider themselves morally superior. There is only one way of owning or even of "having" a cat. And it is the good way.

Last night I heard the first katydid of the season. I do not suppose that one can "have" a katydid even in the sense that I have a frog. Indeed I don't suppose anyone could even love a katydid or any other insect except, of course, in the sense that it has sometimes been supposed that God loves men—which is to say that He loves the race and wishes it well, in general and as a whole, without concerning Himself too much about any individual. I should very much regret the disappearance of all katydids, even of all those who inhabit this particular region. But I can't be very much exercised over the fate of any particular one. Two-legged creatures we are supposed to love as well as we love ourselves. The four-legged, also, can come to seem pretty important. But six legs are too many from the human standpoint. Nothing that has them can be regarded with any sense of great intimacy. I have been known, on occasion, when a katydid wandered down from the tree-tops where they usually stay and fell under my hand, to toss it casually to the pet ducks on the lawn. The lucky duck was grateful, but the insect might find the act strange, coming from a lover of Nature. After all, the ducks could eat corn.

A friend, learned in such matters, tells me that St. Thomas Aquinas answers the plaints of individuals who consider themselves ill-used by God because they are not so strong, or so rich, or so fortunate as most people, by assuring them that the Creation was an Act of Generosity, not an Act of Justice. This means, as I understand it, that no one can claim anything as a right. Life itself is more than he had any reason to expect, and the recipient of bounty has no right to complain that another pauper was given more than he. I confess that I find this a little hard to take so far as I myself am concerned. But I expect the katydid on the way to the duck to understand it. He has had his life up to now. Besides, the duck is bipedal if not *implumis,* and he has the superior claim.

These are complacent August thoughts; jungle thoughts some might call them. And perhaps, considering Nature's state at the moment, they have every right to be. I have never been south of the Tropic of Cancer and therefore have never seen a real jungle; but descriptions often warn us that it is green and somnolent—not, as the imagination tends to picture it, lively or colorful. And in a year like this one, when rain has been superabundant, a New England summer produces a kind of jungle, or at least something a good deal more like one than the August farther south or, *a fortiori,* like the summer in the more arid west, where heat means a sharp decline in vegetative growth and produces something that suggests the desert rather than the jungle.

In our part of the country, where roadsides and fields have been kept artificially clear, there is even in the Jungletime of August the color of sturdy weeds. But these, or at least the abundance of them, is the result of unintentional cultivation. They have taken advantage of our clearings, and many—the goldenrod for example —are doubtless far more prevalent than they were before the white man came. But in the woods and the thickets where Nature has her own way, there is nothing but a jungle of leaves and branches almost as green, almost as thick, and almost as unrelieved as anything the tropics could produce.

As in the jungle itself, something is flourishing wherever sunlight can fall, and we feel, as we never do in spring, that there is too much; an unnecessary repetition of the same thing, so blindly superabundant as to be almost frightening. What is the good of so much life which seems about to choke itself? Green, the most wonderful of all colors, is by now monotonous; is revealed as only the crude, fundamental stuff of a too exuberant life. The quaint fancy which led someone long ago to give one of our common birds a verb for a name—*vireo*, "I am green"—seems inevitable now. "I am green," "I am green, " "I am green," seems all that Nature herself can say at this moment.

Only we, who look before and after, know that this is not the real jungle; that it is merely a phase during which our temperate world puts on its very respectable imitation and shows us what it could do if given the time. We can hardly imagine that the trees will ever be bare and the ground dead again. But we know what we cannot realize; know that all this exuberance will wither in a deadly breath when autumn strikes. Because we do know it, certain sights and certain voices now putting in their first appearance seem ominous, though they are gay enough in themselves.

There is, for example, the small matter of that katydid. Only long weeks of heat have brought him around to the amorous mood which made the peepers vocal nearly five months ago while they were still immersed in ice-water and thus undergoing, without effect, a sovereign, monkish remedy. For the katydid this is, in a sense, spring at last. But we know that once he has started to sing, the day is not far off when we shall hear the last hardy individual of his species, barely able to shake off the numbing effects of cold, dragging out a few last chirps. His first song is, for us if not for him, less the beginning of something than a warning that a season is getting near its end.

So too there is something ominous about the various kinds of wild asters which begin to attract attention about the time the katydid begins to sing. They hint of the end though they are gay in themselves. Or are they, really? Through all its shades they repeat one color and that is the color of mourning. Their blooming is part of a grand ceremony, part of what is called in France (there usually with some tinge of exaggeration) the *pompes funèbres*. Someone is hanging purple on the doorpost of a summer.

September

For Whom the Leaf Falls

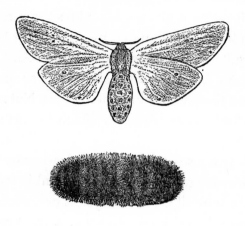

"Hurrying along like a caterpillar in the fall" is said to be—or to have been—a colloquial expression. I do not remember that I ever heard it from the lips of any speaker, but I know very well the creature who must have suggested the comparison. There are not many caterpillars about at this time of year for most kinds have either retired into a chrysalis or a cocoon to spend the winter or long ago turned into a moth or a butterfly which left eggs to survive the snows as best they may. There is, however, one common and conspicuous little fellow, very hairy in appearance and broadly banded in black and red-brown, who is plentiful enough and certainly does hurry along as though he needed to get somewhere quick.

September

As a matter of fact he does. People who notice sometimes call him "woolly bear" or "harlequin caterpillar,"
and this is rather a pity for he enjoys the rare privilege
of being officially designated by a name not jaw-break-
ing but quite euphonious: *Isia isabella*. And whatever
you call him, his air of *empressement* has more justifi-
cation than that of most human hurriers. Not much time
is left to find a cozy corner in which to curl up for the
winter.

Why he chooses to spend the dead season in what
looks like a dangerous and uncomfortable way instead
of shutting himself up in a chrysalis or a cocoon probably no one will ever know. But that is what he has been
doing for some millions of years, and the insects are
conservative in a more thoroughgoing way than a
human being can hope to imitate. When they insist that
the old ways are best, they do not mean the ways of
their youth, or of their fathers' day or even of their
grandfathers'. They may mean the ways of the car-
boniferous age or even before.

In the spring, if all goes well, *Isia isabella* will come
out of hibernation and hurry along again as fast as he
did in the fall because, once again, he can hardly meet
the schedule imposed upon him by the rhythm of his
own physiological process. He will snatch a little food
—preferably a leaf of the plantain you have been careless enough to allow on your lawn—and then resign
himself into a cocoon within which most of his body

will dissolve before re-forming itself. Then he will emerge as a pretty enough little moth, pink and cream in color, but rather less striking than he was in his fur coat.

It is the air of urgency itself which strikes a responsive chord in me when I see him on a garden path in late September. His consciousness, if any, must be dim. He cannot know why he is in a hurry, only that he is. But I recognize in myself a similar vague uneasiness. My preparations for the winter have been made. My house is tight; there is fuel oil in the tank and some food in the cellar. But the confidence of summer has imperceptibly faded. Something impends.

When I was a boy I used to attribute this feeling of uneasiness to the knowledge that I would soon be going unwillingly to school again. As a matter of fact I still have to do just that, and perhaps this is part of the reason why something within me begins to grow tense. But it is certainly no more than a factor or even a rationalization. *Isia isabella* and I know in our nerves and our muscles that something pretty drastic is going to happen and we are not sure that the most we can do about it will be enough.

No doubt individual human beings vary in their psychology almost as much as the kinds of animals do. Your squirrel, for example, is stimulated into a fever of activity in autumn. He is excitable and irascible, quarreling with his fellows and taking time out to scold indignantly any two- or four-footed creature who invades his woods. But he is exuberant rather than hurried or uneasy. He seems confident that his store of nuts will hold out. Similarly many housewives burst into an autumn flurry of activity almost as remarkable as that of the spring, and some of them seem to enjoy it. Some men, even some of those whose desire to be useful about the house is sporadic, are suddenly inspired to take down screens and to put up storm windows. It is as though such purposeful activity released some tensions; as if it relieved, by yielding to them, some urges that rise in time with the rhythm of all Nature. "I feel it," says the subconsciousness; "something is going to happen." "Well," it answers itself, "I am doing something about it, aren't I?"

One day the first prematurely senile leaf will quietly detach itself in a faint breeze and flutter silently to the ground. All through the summer an occasional unnoticed, unregretted leaf has fallen from time to time. But not as this one falls. There is something quietly ominous about the way in which it gives up the ghost, without a struggle, almost with an air of relief. Others will follow, faster, and faster. Soon the ground will be covered, though many of the stubborner trees are still clothed. Then one night a wind, a little harder than usual, and carrying perhaps the drops of a cold rain, will come. We shall awake in the morning to see that the show is over. The trees are naked; bare, ruined choirs, stark against the sky.

To me there always seems to be something perverse about those country dwellers who like the autumn best. Their hearts, I feel, are not in the right place. They must be among those who see Nature merely as a spectacle or a picture, not among those who share her own moods. Spring is the time for exuberance, autumn for melancholy and regret. Season of mists and mellow fruitfulness? Yes, of course, it is that too. But promise, not fulfillment, is what lifts the heart. Autumn is no less fulfillment than it is also the beginning of the inevitable end.

No doubt the colors of autumn are as gorgeous in their own way as any of spring. Looked at merely as color, looked at with the eye of that kind of painter to whom only color and design are important, I suppose they are beautiful and nothing more. But looked at as outward and visible signs, as an expression of what is going on in the world of living things, they produce another effect.

"No spring nor summer beauty hath such grace as I have seen in one autumnal face"—so wrote John Donne in compliment to an old lady. But Donne was enamored of death. Send not to know for whom the leaf falls, it falls for thee.

September

To the physicist, red and green are primary colors. So are they also to the biologist, though in a different sense. They are the primary colors of life—the red of blood and the green of chlorophyll. Your animal keeps his primary color hidden. When we actually see it, open and naked, we shudder. If he flaunted his blood as vegetation flaunts its chlorophyll, if the animal sang red, red, red, as the plant sings green, green, green, it would be intolerable.

Man is conspicuously the connoisseur; presumably he alone experiments consciously with his sensations and learns to play delicately with the pleasure which is almost pain and the harmony which is almost discord. Perhaps that is the reason why he is almost the only animal whose blood shows clearly through the delicate skin, hinting that it flows red, red, red just below the covering just as the clothing of a woman hints of nakedness beneath. But, through the summer at least, the vegetable kingdom has known no such modesty. And because green is as cool as red is hot, we call the summer's leafiness calm and refreshing, indifferent to the fact that it is, in its own way, flaunting the crude stuff of its kind of life.

The colors of autumn are very different from that. Sometimes we think of them as brilliant but that is because we forget their true significance. Autumn colors, russet and yellow, are not primary colors in either the physicist's or the biologist's sense; not the colors of living but of dying. They mean, so the physiologist assures us, not that something has been added, but that something has been taken away. The thrifty tree has withdrawn into its permanent trunk the vital parts worth saving, and it delicately discards something that it would no longer be able to maintain. Spring was the time of expansion, this of retrenchment. There is nothing to do now but to lay low and hope for the best.

Most of us, as well as a great many of the creatures who feel the little premonitory shudder brought by autumn's first breath, will survive. Once our confidence has returned we will rejoice in a new way and take our pleasure in being snug, in feeling ourselves survive, even when the snow and the ice and the cold forbid us to do more than that. We even call the first chill of autumn "bracing," though the very choice of the adjective means something. It is against a stress or a blow that we "brace" ourselves, and no one ever needed to feel "braced" in the springtime. The pleasures we promise ourselves are those of effort and struggle. It will be the season for the stoic and the puritan as spring and summer were the season for the pagan.

Of such pleasures more anon. I should not like to miss them; would not live if I could amid perpetual leaf and bloom, if only because I should miss the emphasis which absence and return alone can contribute. But the little tremor of fear when the first leaf falls is no less real than is the twinge of regret at the beginning of the end of something which had been vivid and rewarding. A very old lady of my acquaintance spoke to her son a few years ago with frank distaste for the winter which was to come. "Well, Mother," he said, "we have managed to endure a good many of them before and I guess we will get through this one, too." "You can if you want," she replied with a good deal of spirit, "but I am not going to." And she didn't. Perhaps we are always reminded that for us too such a time will some day come. Perhaps that realization adds something to our sense of uneasiness.

And what of those very many creatures, among the insects especially, who know but one spring; for whom the fall is not a period of danger, of hardship, or of sleep, but inevitably the end which it has been for all their kind during millions of years? The little, delicate, pale-green tree-crickets, for instance, who have sung so persistently for a few weeks and produced a volume of sound so incredibly great in proportion to their size. In their heyday they kept well under cover and were almost impossible to locate even when they were making their near presence conspicuous. Now they seem to gather in companies on the trunk of my apple tree waiting for the anaesthetizing chill.

Occasionally, also, you may see a solitary individual of this or some other short-lived species who has survived a little longer than he should. He moves sluggishly, perhaps utters an occasional low cheep, and moves into the failing warmth of the autumn sun like one of those last human survivors of a universal calamity whom imaginative writers have pictured as hopelessly prolonging life on a cooling planet which will never grow warm again. For these creatures the fact that spring will return in six or eight months is a fact as useless as it would be for a man in similar position who knew that the earth was to become habitable again in a million years. Indeed, our tree-cricket or our katydid would not live much longer if we moved him into artificial warmth and supplied him with food from our larder. He has got into the habit of dying at about this time. His whole life scheme is adjusted to the brevity of the season which favors him. Like a very old man he seems to die of nothing except death itself.

Of course such an insect does not know that he is going to die in the sense that a man can know that his end is imminent. Perhaps, indeed, even a man cannot really know that; cannot really grasp what it means. And the man has a brain, the insect a nerve mechanism so different from ours that it is infinitely more unlike that of the stupidest mammal than the brain of that stupidest mammal is unlike ours. Yet even sober and objective naturalists have been unable at times to refrain from speculating over the meaning of what we can only call, by inappropriate human analogy, the insect's "attitude toward death"—and especially of that attitude as it affects, or rather fails to affect, his obsession with the future welfare of his species. Men often say of an object or of an institution, or of their house or their government, or even of the solar system itself: "Well, I guess it will last out my time, and that is enough for me." But an insect would be as incapable of acting on that principle as he would be of saying he was going to.

Men, to be sure, commonly care about the welfare of their children. But they have seen those children and established some relation with them, whereas in the vast majority of cases the insect never sees his offspring and, in the case of many many species—for instance, that of the crickets and grasshoppers we have been talking about—is dead the whole aeon of a winter before his children will hatch in the spring he can never see. It is true that the ants, the bees, and the wasps do actually take care of grubs which they seem surprisingly to recognize as potentially creatures like themselves; true, also, that some other multilegged beasts have some association with their young—as in the somehow repulsive case of the large wolf spider whom many have seen wandering abroad with the whole pullulating mass of her spiderlings piled on her back. But the rule is that eggs are laid and then abandoned; that, very frequently indeed, they are not hatched until long after the parent has succumbed to cold or to old age. And yet there is no business to which insects are so passionately devoted as to that of preparing, often very elaborately indeed, for the welfare of this progeny. It is very much as though a man were to consider it his chief business in life to arrange for the well-being, not of his children, but of some distant descendants a thousand years removed from him.

From this extraordinary fact many different morals, no doubt all of them inadmissible, have been drawn. To some it has seemed that the obvious conclusion is this: Since the insects cannot possibly know what they are doing, God must. He tells them what to do and they do it, though only He knows why. Others have used the same facts to reproach man with his selfishness; with his inability to be as much concerned about posterity as a grasshopper is.

Even George Bernard Shaw could think of no better approach to our difficulties than the suggestion that we should all learn to live as long as Methuselah so that we would simply have to care about more of the future than we short-lived animals can now care. But consider, if you can, the sense of responsibility which dominates the creatures of one short summer. Men have often been told that they ought to face death calmly, secure in the knowledge that life will go on; been told that they can feel this fact most intimately in connection with their own children. But does the argument really work, for us? Seldom, I imagine, so well as it works for either the katydid who dies in September, or the bee who has gladly busied himself into exhaustion in six short weeks and died even in the midst of the honey-flow.

The ego of these creatures, their individualism, if you like, is more than under control; it is nonexistent. Here are your perfect citizens of the world state and the classless society. Automatically they consider the welfare of the race above their own, and they do not mind even if a thousand of their children die; do not mind even if—as is said to be the case with the wolf spider—some of their children eat the others up; provided only that a sufficient number survive. In respect to them, as in respect to some human zealots devoted to the cause of humanity at large, it is sometimes hard to tell where a laudable concern with the greatest good of the greatest number leaves off and mere brutality begins. Tennyson reproached Nature because: "So careful of the type she seems, so careless of the single life." He did not suggest that we should imitate her. But that is precisely what these insects do.

Just how far this is admirable and worthy of imitation I leave an open question. I have, however, less doubt about what is a merely negative aspect of the situation—the calmness, I mean, with which our katydid seems to accept the inevitable when autumn does come. That acceptance appears to be more absolute than that of even the lower warm-blooded animals, but, even so, most creatures except man seem largely exempt from mere fretful fear and from useless protest. Gustav Eckstein has remarked that though we often speak of animals as "going away to die," the fact seems to be simply that they go away, not to die but to be ill—in peace and in quiet. But many observers have commented on what seems to be the fact that fear plays a much smaller part than we should think it must in the life of an animal who lives dangerously. Terror he can know, and perhaps he knows it frequently. But it seems to last only a little longer than the immediate danger which it helps him to avoid, instead of lingering, as in the human being it does, until it becomes itself a burden and a threat. The frightened bird resumes his song as soon as danger has passed, and so does the frightened rabbit his games. It is almost as though they knew that "Cowards die many times before their deaths; the valiant never taste of death but once."

To accuse his fate and to rail against it, is man's dubious prerogative. Few would be willing to deny it to themselves but it is not attractive in others. And that, certainly, is one of the reasons why the fellowship with animals who, for the most part, will not compete with us in lamentations, is so agreeable. Sometimes the cornered beast will seem to plead with his eyes, and perhaps he actually does so. For the most part, however, the interventions of man seem to be accepted as a portion of impersonal fate, and only the domesticated ani-

mals clearly and persistently reproach us—as the cat
who has not been fed or the dog who has been scolded
often does. Your wild four-footed creature crawls away
to die quietly; your bird, so I am told, often simply stops
in the midst of a flight and falls to the ground; your
katydid seems merely to drop as the autumn leaf does.

Only the tree puts on a spectacular display and that
is in honor of only a temporary death, not a permanent
one. But at least the leaf which assumes its astonishing
though sober color is doing so in honor of its own end,
and there is something about the process which suggests our own attempts to be brave "in the infamy of our
natures." Logan Pearsall Smith once remarked that, so
far as he was concerned, the only consolation which
words had ever afforded him in face of the thought of
death was not the consolation offered by philosophy,
or science, or religion, but simply that which poetry or
any magnificent utterance is able to convey by the very
fact that it can be magnificent on such a theme. The
colors of autumn seem to be accomplishing something
very much like that; seem to be saying "moriturus"
grandly. "The bright day is done and we are for the
dark."

October

Autumn Overturn

There is a curious difference between the end of summer and the beginning of winter. Last month Nature and I were vaguely apprehensive. A vast change was imminent which we resisted and resented. Now the tide has turned, a crucial moment has definitely passed. The inevitable has been accepted and it turns out not to be so bad. We no longer expect trees to be green or the air merely caressing. Growth is no longer taken for granted. There is a pause and we have got used to standing still. We look forward instead of back, and winter, which once seemed inconceivable, now promises pleasure of its own.

October

All this has happened because a few weeks ago the sun "crossed the equator"—if one may fall into that turn of speech which is no more arrogantly anthropocentric than the usual statement "The sun has risen" or "The sun has set." Paradoxically, the earth has meanwhile been moving closer to the great source of all heat as the temperature fell, and it will be closest of all in late December. But in our hemisphere proximity is more than compensated for by the fact that we are turned more and more away from the sun, so that its light falls upon us more and more obliquely, and for fewer and fewer hours per day.

That much of what has been going on is the part of the process which is steady and continuous; which proceeds with clocklike—or, rather, with more than clocklike—regularity. Here on our globe, on the other hand, the phenomena which depend ultimately upon the mechanical movements of the heavenly bodies seem to take their own time, to be almost humanly capricious, as though they were refusing to admit their dependence and preferred to pretend that they were simply going their own way. "Don't hurry me" is what autumn seems to say as she brings a bright, warm, almost springlike day to follow a dark and chilly one.

If we had forgotten all previous falls or if we were destined, like some creatures, to know but one, we might have recurrent doubts whether the slow change we had been observing was real. Then comes a day, colder than any experienced before, and we know that despite all its deceptive rallies the one season is yielding and the other coming on. If the earth has resisted, it is only in that limited fashion in which, some determinists say, human individuals and human society can resist what some call "fate" and some "history." Even, so they say, if there is no straight-line movement toward the inevitable, the zigzag line leads there, ineluctably. So far as the seasons and the cycles are concerned, this earth of ours enjoys no more freedom than the old astrologers allowed the human being. The pull of the stars was irresistible at last though we might get to our appointed end slowly or rapidly, with interludes or without them.

Living creatures take advantage of the lagging and the capriciousness. It lengthens out their time of preparation and adjustment and there is more being done than even the observer of such things can ever quite grasp. Many many creatures besides the obvious squirrel are laying up stores which are no less important to them though their whole autumn harvest may amount to less than half a thimbleful. Many others besides the chipmunk and the woodchuck have disappeared, or soon will disappear, into hibernation. The milk snakes and the garter snakes and the comically bluffing little puff adders are crawling away into rock crevices. Those of the insects which elect to pass the winter as adults are creeping under stones, or, like certain eccentric butterflies, choosing the place—a rafter in a barn perhaps—where they will remain almost motionless for month after month. The toads are digging in; the frogs and turtles burying themselves in the mud; and if the swallows are not, as Dr. Samuel Johnson was by no means the only one to believe, "conglobulating" in preparation for a plunge beneath the waters of some pond, they are doing something equally remarkable—namely, flying far away.

Even below the level of these perhaps wholly instinctive and therefore perhaps not consciously purposive activities are others in ourselves and in other animals which are certainly not consciously willed. The fur of those four-footed creatures who do not sleep the winter through is mysteriously growing longer and the warm layer of fat under the skin is growing thicker. Indeed, even inanimate things are taking part in the cyclical reorganization. This, for instance, is for lakes and ponds the time of what limnologists call "the autumn overturn"; one of the two annual revolutions which betray how even the elemental substances must react to the fact that the earth's axis is inclined out of the plane of its annual revolution.

If water were like the vast majority of known liquids and contracted steadily as it grew colder so that it got steadily heavier and heavier, then no such phenomenon would occur. But because water gets heavier only as the temperature descends almost to freezing and then

grows lighter again before it actually turns into ice,
every body of inland water turns over twice a year—in
the spring because the surface, though warmer than the
depth, is actually heavier and so sinks; in the autumn,
because a reverse series of changes takes place. And a
good thing that is, too, because, so meteorologists tell
us, if water did not have this almost unique quality,
then ice, even in the temperate regions, would freeze
so thick that it would be hardly melted by the end of
summer, and most life, as we know it in those regions,
would be impossible. "This," say some, "is another and
particularly striking proof of the fact that the earth
was intelligently designed. Water cannot have 'evolved'
this characteristic. God gave to it, to the liquid He intended principally to employ, the peculiar qualities
which would make it useful for its purpose." "This,"
say others, "is only another example of the way in which
life has adapted itself to, and taken advantage of, the
conditions which it found." You may take your choice.

Even we complicated creatures who have attempted
in so many and such ingenious ways to declare our independence of the seasons, and even of Nature as a
whole, respond more fundamentally than we know to
her rhythms. As surely as the squirrel, we make—or
more characteristically have someone else make for us—
certain preparations for the winter. Moreover, though
we do not grow more hairy, or, with any dependable

regularity, fatter, a doctor friend tells me that the chemical composition of my blood changes in fall and spring. I have my own seasonal overturn. And I am wondering if the reason why winter seems less alarming now that it is almost here than it did when I looked at it from summer across the intervening autumn may not be, in part, that my blood was not then, as it is now, winter blood. I am prepared for cold as I was then prepared for heat, but I had not sufficient faith that it would be so.

Now in October I begin to feel myself akin, not with the katydid who dies or the woodchuck who hibernates, but with the squirrels and the mice and the foxes, who stay awake. Whole new troops of birds arrive and I remind myself that the appearance of a flock of juncos is as true and as significant a sign of autumn as the falling of the leaf. Some of the birds will only pass by on their way to milder climates; but for others, as for the junco, this is a winter resort, a place where all real rigors may be escaped.

I notice, too, that we hardier folk draw closer together. During the summer I rarely saw the chickadees, who are nevertheless permanent residents. They had scattered to the woods on business of their own, especially the business of building nests in the tree hollows. Now they come closer to the house and resume their habit of chirping amiably when I pass near them. Only the other day I saw a squirrel a few feet from the door, a common enough sight in winter but a rare one at the height of the warm season. Before long I shall hear some evening a skunk or a 'possum sniffing about the house.

New York City is less than seventy-five miles away and this is a rather thickly settled community. Skunks and 'possums are not "protected." Most of my neighbors do not consider them desirable residents. They shoot them when they get a chance and they would pass zoning ordinances against them if they could. But I like them as well as the much more fiercely persecuted woodchuck, which manages to flourish, I am glad to say. In fact, the case of the 'possum gives me a very deep satisfaction.

He is not, to put it gently, a very intelligent animal, and not (by any standards except those of another 'possum) a very handsome one. Moreover, among his characteristics is one which, for some obscure reason, most human beings find it difficult to forgive—a hairless tail. Few will be very much moved if I add in his favor that he is the only North American marsupial, for most people, I suppose, would regard this as a possibly valid reason for keeping him in a zoo, though not for having him on the lawn. But for all his stupidity—and he is rather stupid—he has put one over on us inheritors of the earth and is actually extending his range. In our grandfathers' time he was never seen about here, never east of the Hudson River. But in southern New England nowadays he is quite common. The human species is not the only one that decides from time to time that it needs more *Lebensraum* and proceeds to take it.

Presently I shall begin to put out food for the birds and for the squirrels too—though this last was not part of my original intention. They came, uninvited, to eat what was meant for others, and during most of one winter we kept up a battle of wits, I devising means of making the food inaccessible, they demonstrating that I was not so smart as I thought. They could leap farther than even I, with considerable respect for their talents in that direction, believed possible, and when I hung receptacles by long cords they promptly—with an air of saying: "Just how stupid do you think we are, anyway?"—pulled up the string, hand over hand, until the food was on the limb beside them.

I won the contest at last with a platform supported on a single high post, incased in new galvanized iron. But it was a hollow victory; I could not harden my heart, and the ultimate result was a second feeder intended especially for the squirrely tribe. Moreover, it was just as well that I gave in, because as soon as the metal on the bird-feeder post rusted a little, it was climbed without difficulty. Since squirrels, though rodents, have hairy tails, they are generally looked on with favor, at least by those human beings who look with favor on any animals at all. I don't suppose they know how much they owe to this accident of Nature. Except for it they would not be tolerated in public parks and instead of peanuts they would be given rough-on-rats.

My reward for having made my arrangements will be a constant reminder, even in the depth of winter, that I am not alone in being still alive and still awake. Without them I should see, even on walks through the snow, comparatively few signs of life; an occasional bird is all that can be counted upon. There would be tracks of course; often the tiny ones that disappear into a snow-tunnel where a white-footed mouse has decided to go under the surface for a while. But I should have to be content merely with knowing what I could not see, for I have not had any luck with an experiment sometimes recommended. I have knocked repeatedly on the trunks of trees which carry, high up, the balls of leaves in which the squirrels spend the less clement days. Yet I have never seen one peer out inquiringly as I have been assured that they would—perhaps because I had already been observed as I approached and the squirrel's curiosity was satisfied. But if I cannot go calling on the animals, they, thanks to the food, come calling on me. At almost any hour of almost any day I can convince myself that the term "dead of winter" is inappropriate. One or more representatives of one or more of the dozen species of birds that come to the feeder is almost sure to be about, and so is anything up to ten or a dozen squirrels—a rather alarming number of the latter, to tell the truth, especially during the days when corn came high.

If I call these squirrels and these birds "friendly creatures," there are, I know, many people who will be ready to accuse me of arrant sentimentality. "Even if," they say, "you don't know that what you call the affection of your cats and other pets is merely their recognition of a good thing when they see one, then at least even you ought to know that it is not your friendship but your food which the squirrels and the birds are after. Even you can hardly have failed to notice how quickly they disappear in the late spring when they need you no longer." But I am not really abashed by such arguments as these and I will not even fall back upon the contention that pets do exhibit what looks as much like affection as anything one commonly meets with in a human being, or that certain wild creatures do seem to show a real liking for the near presence of our kind. Grant fully the dominance of the interested motives and I can still say only that I am not so sure of the complete purity of my own as to demand it in the animals.

I do not mean this as simple and obvious cynicism. I am not saying flatly that everyone is out to get what he can, nor am I merely attempting the paradoxical all-men-would-be-cowards-if-they-dared gambit. I am only saying that "liking" and "loving" are both very complex things which are impossible to separate entirely from a kind of profit motive. When we "like" a fellow creature, we may, if we are very generous persons, want to pay him back with disproportionate lavishness for what he has given us in pleasure or profit; but we would not have liked him to begin with, would not have been moved to generosity, if he had not given us something in the first instance, even though that was no more than the beauty and the charm of his presence.

I see no reason to suppose that when my cat rubs himself against my legs—even if it is when mealtime is near—he is being merely hypocritical. The love he has for me is certainly not unconnected with the fact that from me various blessings have flowed. But can we deny that the warm glow which suffuses us when we anticipate a meeting with a friend or a loved one has a very great deal to do with the pleasure we anticipate in the meeting? There is the prospect of a good dinner at a friend's house, the prospect of the illumination of his talk, perhaps of the stimulation provided by the mere presence of a beautiful woman. Could one very well "like" a physically repulsive bore who fed one badly or not at all? And if not, then why expect more of any of the creatures whom, nevertheless, we insist upon describing as "lower" than we are? Perhaps we can pity those who give us nothing, and perhaps—if we can really do that—we do something which only a man can do. But bald pity is not love.

There is also, of course, said to be a kind of love characteristic of some parents and of some amorists which grows on neglect and on abuse, which loves a child or a member of the opposite sex *because* he is not lovable. But surely that is often close in man, if not perhaps in God, to perversity; and ordinarily the most we can expect in human beings is the absence of mere hypocrisy and of a too careful calculation of the balance between what we get and what we give. As for the squirrels and the birds, their motives are no doubt pretty direct and fairly simple. They are happy to dine with me and happiness is itself a kind of gratitude, even though in their case they may feel no more than we feel for those of our acquaintance whose chief claim on our affections is the atmosphere created in their houses by the sure prospect of a good dinner.

Of the cat, on the other hand, I am by no means sure that this is all that can be said. Sometimes he cajoles with a direct aim in view—and who does not do the same? But there are other times when he wants nothing except to say that he likes me and likes me to like him in return. His gratitude for past favors has diffused itself into that warm glow of liking which is probably as much as most of us manage most of the time. On the whole it seems to me that both cats and dogs repay favors with love at least as abundantly as human beings usually do.

October

I have noticed that, as a class, it is the rich who are especially anxious to be loved for themselves alone. The fact is understandable since they are no doubt particularly likely to be imposed upon. But it tends to become an obsession and it is one of their less attractive traits. If, as I suppose, they find it hard to love anyone who is suspected of directly interested motives, they nevertheless come, in the end, to suffer from the fact that it is hard to be loved if you yourself are afraid of giving any solid motive to those who otherwise might love you.

No doubt that is one of the reasons why even the philanthropic rich are so likely to avoid direct benefits to individuals, are so prone to hedge their gifts about with provisions which make it impossible for any designing person to profit directly from them. If they can get no direct expression of gratitude from the city which is given a public library, then at least (so they feel) they escape the humiliation of being thanked by someone who would only be hoping for more. Mr. George Eastman, I was told by one who had had a good deal of contact with him, committed suicide partly because he lived in the growing conviction that no one ever came to see him except with an ulterior motive. Perhaps he would have been happier if he had not been so determined not to be victimized.

At any rate I am determined, in my relations with the animal inhabitants of the township where I live, not

October

to suffer as Mr. Eastman suffered. It is my intention to continue to feed the birds and the squirrels without worrying too much over the question whether or not they love me "for myself alone." I am not even sure that they should.

November

This Middle State

Last week I had a visitor from the city and I am afraid that both of us were relieved when Monday morning came round at last. It has happened before, but neither of us can learn—or, more probably, can admit that he has learned. Under other circumstances we get along very well indeed. I respect him and I find him entertaining. I rather believe that he would say the same of me. But "Nature puts him out." I think that there have been moments when he was on the point of suggesting that we pull down the shades.

What makes the case of this particular friend interesting is the fact that his aversion is a genuine aversion, not merely a negative failure to be interested in what

November

Nature has to offer. Your average city dweller, whether he be intellectual or merely cockney, can take a country week end in his stride; in fact may even enjoy it as an interlude. So far as possible he brings the city with him; comes loaded with bottles, possibly with books or magazines, and with the paraphernalia of some organized sport. What he dreads is mere emptiness, mere lack of occupation, and even with these artificial aids he cannot face more than a few days for the simple reason that his normal activities are interrupted and his normal interests no longer fed.

Such a man may be pitied, but there is nothing very mysterious or very interesting about his case. I know many such. Some of them actually own houses in the country, and sometimes genuinely believe that they are fond of what they innocently call "country life." But the friend of whom I am thinking at the moment belongs in quite another class. The one sort thinks he is indifferent to or even that he likes the out-of-doors because he does not really know what the out-of-doors is; my friend dislikes it, dislikes Nature herself, just because he does know—or at least senses—what she is and what she means.

He has never spoken, as another friend sometimes does, of his eagerness to get back to "God's concrete," but I know that he feels it. Even as he steps off the train at our rather bustling little station, he looks about warily as though he half expected to see hostile Indians, and by the time our automobile has stopped in front of my garage, he is definitely alarmed. He knows that I am not really going to ask him to clear the forest or, for that matter, to go for a walk. But the surroundings suggest the theoretical possibility of such things and they make him uneasy.

Outdoors in the summertime he tolerates my small lawn and mildly approves of the few flowers carefully confined to their beds. They are like the caged animals in a zoo, put on exhibition to satisfy public curiosity and therefore well enough in their way. But why, just beyond the confines of this lawn, are all these other trees and shrubs and herbs allowed, as it were, to run around loose? I do not think that he anticipates any definable danger from a bit of wild laurel or even from a squirrel, but they are obviously out of place. My modest little woodland, mostly unimpressive second growth, carries the threat, vague but disturbing, of the immemorial forest pushing in to surround him.

My friend has, in other words, got used to the assumption that Nature has been tamed, that even plants are things that grow when, and only when, they are tended in pots on a window-sill or a penthouse terrace. They are, in their way, as safe as pekinese or poodles. But out here they are actually growing on their own. I do not water them; the rain does. They do not even ask my permission to grow. They have a will and a competent self-reliance of their own. To what may such a state of affairs possibly lead? Just how safe are we against the possibility of a sort of revolt of the Helots? If Nature looks as though she might be capable of seizing a favorable opportunity to take over, then he would prefer to be somewhere else. New York City might have time to prepare her defense while Connecticut was being engulfed.

This time I asked him to come in November because I thought the relatively dead season might prove reassuring. His enemies have even the season as their enemy. The chill blasts have given the impudent weeds and the bold, arrogant trees their come-uppance. The animals are lying low and we can stay in the house. We can keep warmer than they can and by means which are reassuringly the same as those of the city. Furnaces burn oil in Connecticut as well as in New York. This room is quite as comfortable as an apartment. Unfortunately, however, the object lesson did not really convince. My friend could not forget last summer's horrors. The trees, though bare, are not dead but sleeping. The hard brown earth may feel a little more like cement than it did before, but life will spring out of it again next May or June. Man does not own this land. The untamed seeds as well as the untamed insects and animal creatures are only biding their time. That time will come again.

And so, on Monday morning, we part, he relieved to be returning to the world where man has successfully imposed himself upon nearly everything which is visible; I happy to be allowed to remain where nearly everything reminds me that I am part of something neither myself nor wholly subject to me. I am not too intolerant of his attitude because I remember that my own was once not so very different, but I realize that we belong now in two different, very significant categories, and that there is no telling to what ultimate extremes either his premise or mine might ultimately lead not only us as two individuals but the whole mass of those who agree with the one or the other.

The Reverend Sydney Smith who bewailed his sad fate when he found himself "twelve miles from a lemon" is the perfect example of the highly intelligent man whose dismay outside city limits is the result of nothing except the mere negative failure to notice that there is anything there even possibly meaningful, for good or for evil. Some of the best of his sayings clearly proclaim that fact. Take, for instance: "I have no relish for the country; it is a kind of healthy grave." Or the remark about living in a place with only one post a day and therefore with no really fresh news: "In the country I always fear that creation will expire before tea-time." His present-day descendants are those who feel the same way if they do not get the latest bulletins by radio, "every hour on the hour." But to them the proper answer is Thoreau's: "I had no idea that there was so much going on in Heywood's meadow," and the real question is: What news is of greatest importance? Is the resurrection significant? If so, then why are there no bulletins to announce that the fat caterpillar who hung his green and gold sarcophagus not far from my study door has emerged in the form of a Monarch butterfly?

No, the real horror of the country for those who can feel it, and feel it as horror, is not the fact that it is empty or that nothing happens, but quite simply that there is so much here which is not man, so much happening here which may concern man deeply if, though only if, he is willing to admit that what does not concern him exclusively may be, for that very reason, far more significant than the things which only he knows about or cares about. If, as Sydney Smith feared, "creation" should come to an end before tea-time, the news would not be published in London any more than it would be published in Yorkshire. What London might know about before the counties did would be the fall of a government, the bombing of a city, perhaps the beginning of the end of "civilization." But "creation" includes a great deal more than what any such man-made catastrophe would put an end to. Thousands of living things would continue to lead what seem to be quite happy existences, entirely unaware that what we like to call the world had come to an end. The cockroach and the bird were both here long before we were. Both could get along very well without us, although it is perhaps significant that of the two the cockroach would miss us more.

I respect the friend to whom I have just said good-bye because he is a true philosophical hater of the country, not merely one who is unaware of its existence or of the fact that it means anything. What distinguishes such true haters from the true lovers is partly the difference in their attitude toward the question whether what goes on in Nature is something to which we should look for some guidance in the attempt to solve our own practical problems, and partly a difference in emotional reaction when the vast world of the living but nonhuman invites our awareness. And of the two it is the second which has more to do with love or hate as pure emotional experiences. Is it comfort as well as excitement which the spectacle provokes, or is it distaste not unmingled with a kind of fear?

No one, so it seems to me, can properly be called either a lover or a hater who does not find himself moved when in Nature's presence by one or the other of these emotions and who does not, to some extent, recognize its source. Without being so moved he may enjoy fresh air and an open space for exercise. He may be glad to get away from crowds and may feel the peace of a successful escape. But if that is all, then he has not advanced beyond the mere Horatian ideal of retirement, has made no contact with Nature in the sense in which those who love her for her own sake understand their love. Perhaps he is even capable of some purely aesthetic pleasure in the shape and color of hills or of trees. But if these are no more than shapes and colors, then he has no communion with anything except himself.

Everywhere, even in November, Nature invites that communion. The bare trees raise their limbs toward heaven and permit us to interpret as well as to share that gesture. It is no mere *de profundis clamavi;* perhaps it is also not either adoration or a plea for intercession. Perhaps instead it is something rather like defiance. "We are alive," say the trees, "and you, O sky, are not. Without your light we would perish; unless the sun comes in time to shed its rays less obliquely upon us, we shall never awake from the sleep which now envelops us. But what you have the power to give, you yourself are without, you can have no share in. You represent the regular, the remorseless, the thing which endures so long that you are, as we count things, eternal. But we are part of the Great Rebellion against your exclusive rule.

"Enclosed within the cellulose walls of the little blocks out of which our great structure is made there is a jelly which is in many respects much more different from man's protoplasm than that protoplasm is from the protozoan jelly; but it is not utterly different. We and the animals took our separate routes long long ago, but we started out together—as man with his micro-scope knows when he discovers under it little creatures that are neither plant nor animal but are both, living things for whom the distinction between flesh and vegetable tissue has as yet no meaning. And we are still, as tree and as man, alike in the very important fact that we are different from stars or suns. You circle in what seems an endless regular dance, you provide for us not only a place to live but also a magnificent spectacle for our enjoyment. But you are without will and without sentience. And we have both. We can, as you cannot, assert ourselves. We are alive, I tell you, we are alive! And at least some of us know that we are."

There is an obvious reason why it may be just as well that most men refuse to consider that contemplation is the final, the only real end of man. If most men did so consider it and had always done so, the result would perhaps be that we should start devoting ourselves too soon and too exclusively to that occupation; too soon because we may even yet not have become capable of contemplating so wisely or so deeply as we some day may. But it is worth noting that the speculative mind finds it difficult to formulate any other ultimate end, any ultimate goal other than that of happy contempla-tion. It was, of course, what Aristotle believed to be the only activity which man could perform better than his fellow creatures, and if it be objected that Aristotle was only one of those ancient Greeks, then there is the strange case of Mr. George Bernard Shaw.

No one ever urged us more insistently to stop mooning about, to get busy and do something. Practically everything ought to be changed—beginning with man himself, and, especially, the absurd brevity of his life span. But when Mr. Shaw himself undertook to tell us what all this changing had in view, and what the really changed man in the really changed world would be doing, he came out with the surprisingly Aristotelian conclusion that his "ancients," grown incredibly wise in their incredibly distant future, will spend their long old age standing about in robes and beards, furiously contemplating the universe. Mr. Shaw would, of course, be the first to protest that all this is still a long way off and that what we have to do now is not to contemplate but to make a world worthy of contemplation. But at least we might start practicing in our own limited way on the material at hand. A life in which there is not at least some contemplation, a life lived without some awareness of life itself, is not a human life at all.

And what then shall we contemplate? My friend who hates the country would, I am sure, answer without any hesitation: "Man and the works of man, including [as I rather suspect he would put it] God." That program does provide considerable scope. At one extreme it includes gossip which is the raw material of the comedy of manners, and from that level it rises to the most abstruse metaphysical speculations—which, as again I rather suspect, my friend regards, not as a method of attaining absolute truth, but simply as a human game played in accordance with the arbitrary rules determining the operations of our mind. But in any event, man is for him the be-all and end-all.

Even if it is true that man somehow evolved from "lower forms of life," these lower forms are part of a shabby past well forgotten. He would, I suppose, admit that those so inclined can learn something *about* the paramecium and the squirrel but not, surely, anything *from* them. To him man may be only:

> Placed on this isthmus of a middle state,
> A being darkly wise and rudely great,

but nothing "below" man is worth thinking about. At best the other animals are no more than poor—and stupid—relations, with whom it would be a waste of time to associate. My fondness for them and my interest in their ways probably strikes him as only a *nostalgie pour la boue,* like that taste for low company which afflicts some otherwise refined and intelligent people.

But is all animate Nature outside man really no more than something that has been left behind, some portions of which are accidentally useful but all of which is a mere survival from an outgrown past? Is the song of a bird or the flowering of a plant merely a lesser thing than we are capable of, merely an obsolete manifestation of the force which has found its only true expression in ourselves? Or are both quite as genuine and quite as nearly ultimate as our own activities are? Do we have any "excuse for being" more convincing than the excuse everything has which is successfully and joyfully alive?

The theory of evolution is an interesting theory and I assume that it corresponds to certain facts. But if it encourages the assumption that all the "lower"—i.e., earlier—forms are merely outmoded, then it is guilty of encouraging the same unfortunate confusion which the scientific approach generally does encourage when it talks about "development" and "improvement" in connection with things which exist for themselves, not in order to serve merely as steppingstones. Mr. Eliot's *The Wasteland* is not "higher" than Homer's *Iliad*, does not render it obsolete. Neither is the dandelion, which belongs to a relatively late and very complex plant family, in every respect an improvement on the orchid, which belongs to an earlier and simpler one. If animate Nature as a whole is more like a work of art than like a machine; if, in a word, each of its manifestations exhibits excellencies of its own; then why should man regard everything that came before him as a step—often a false step—on the road up to him? Who, indeed, if he ever actually allowed himself to become aware of an animal or a plant, could ever entertain any such idea? Full many a flower is born to blush unseen, but if it could be consulted it would hardly agree that its fragrance was wasted. It had had its moments, whether or not any of us happened to be there to see or to smell.

The distinction between learning *about* and learning *from* is, I am sure, the crucial one, and any science which proposes for itself nothing but the first is dead; can be no more than a branch of practical mechanics; can accomplish none but utilitarian purposes. It furnishes no subject for contemplation; it contracts rather than enlarges the understanding; it impoverishes rather than enriches the emotional life of man. *From* Nature we learn what we are a part of and how we may participate in the whole; we gain a perspective on ourselves which serves, not to set us aside from, but to put us in relation with, a complex scheme. Perhaps we also learn to suspect that we too are our own excuse for being, born to blush unseen by any eyes except eyes like our own.

Historical accounts make it clear enough that when Darwin and Huxley won their battle over *The Origin of Species* and *The Descent of Man,* the most they achieved was a reluctant, shamefaced confession that man is a part of Nature and must admit his blood relationship with other living things—very much as a proud family might admit, when faced with the evidence of some genealogist, that it has had its obscure and humble branches.

No doubt this was in part because the popular mind

made the issue simply the question whether or not the caged ape in the zoo was to be recognized as a brother; and perhaps its attitude might have been different if it had realized—as comparatively few seem to realize even today—that it was not having foisted upon it some disreputable "poor relation" but offered, instead, admission into a great fellowship: the privilege of considering itself a part of Nature's great family. And if the thing had been seen in that light, then perhaps mankind would have been ready, not merely to admit, but proudly to claim, its privilege.

On this earth, perhaps throughout the whole universe, the most fundamental of all antimonies, the most crucial of all struggles is that between life and death—or, as it might be more true to say, between life and not-life. And who, capable of realizing this fact, or of seeing himself as part of the Great Rebellion of the animate against the inanimate, can fail to find comfort in the fact that it is not alone in him that the one protagonist is embodied; perhaps even that the ultimate issues do not depend upon his success or his failure alone? Consider again the November trees which lift their arms to say that they have only temporarily yielded; that next spring they will again assert their determination to live. Those trees, like the frog now sleeping under the mud, are on our side.

December

First Snow

There are certain things which children should not be allowed to see too soon—such things, I mean, as the sea, the mountains, and, above all, the snow. To a child all phenomena are equally remarkable and therefore not remarkable at all. The most astonishing are taken for granted before he knows that they oughtn't to be. I have long envied those who never saw so much as even one flake of crystal until a day when—after they had reached years of discretion—they were permitted to watch the whole visible earth disappear under the relentless accumulation of soft, glistening powder. No matter how hard I try, I know that I shall never be able to see a snowfall with really fresh eyes; that I can never shake off completely the dulling effect of the fact that I have always known from my own experience that such things do happen. Not even the first sight of the ocean, not even a first glimpse of the Jungfrau, granted to eyes which had never before beheld anything except the plains of Kansas, could produce such an effect.

More than one writer, I believe, has wondered if the moths and the butterflies do not have a better design for living than we. In the inconceivably deep sleep of the chrysalis, during which most of their body substance is broken down to be used anew, they no doubt forget their humble and restricted lives as mere crawling things. Suddenly they awake to winged maturity, wholly alive and alert, as competent as they will ever be to act and to experience. Anatole France, I remember, especially—and characteristically—envied them a summer of dancing and love wholly freed in many instances from even the necessity of sucking nectar. The best, he thought, should be reserved for the last, and it would be far better if we too could have a careless youth at the end of our lives. For youth, as Mr. Shaw once remarked, is too good a thing to be wasted on the young.

But I do not remember ever to have heard advanced the other argument pointing in the same direction—the suggestion, I mean, that the butterfly also has over us the advantage of first seeing the world when he is ready to appreciate it, that he is spared the dulling effect of experience upon us who came as children matter-of-factly to accept what, for that reason, we shall never truly see. Only Adam had the privilege of first looking at the world through eyes capable of wonder, and perhaps Adam was the only man who could ever have appreciated the miracle of the snow for the miracle that it actually is. And Adam, alas, was born into a paradise less paradisiac than it might have been if snow had been permitted to fall in the Euphrates Valley.

That from the sky itself this inexhaustible whiteness should descend, often gently but always relentlessly, until the earth has been transformed on a scale that the boldest of engineers would not dream of attempting to imitate! That in one night more cubic yards should be laid down than were moved in the years when the Panama Canal was a-building! We awake to find that the whole visible world has been regraded and landscaped anew. But so neatly as well as so grandly, too! Where is the mess that our operations always involve, where the rubbish and the disorder? Every detail is finished. There is not a curve not graceful, not a form not pleasing.

Only yesterday this miracle was promised for New England. The daily papers said merely: "Tonight—snow." And when I looked out of the window this morning I wondered if such a masterpiece of understatement had, on any other occasion, ever been achieved by journalism. "MAYOR DENOUNCES HIS OPPONENTS," "THRILLING GANG FILM AT THE COLISEUM," "HIGHWAY DEPARTMENT WILL WIDEN CHESTNUT STREET" . . . and then: "Tonight—snow." I am sure that *The Daily Universe,* wherever it may be published, would estimate differently how much display each of these stories was worth.

How utterly all our attempts to deal decoratively with the theme succeed only in making it trivial! We hang bits of cotton on our Christmas trees and buy greeting cards sprinkled with bits of mica. Jingle bells, jingle bells! But perhaps even this is an acknowledgment of the fact that where the best is absurdly inadequate, the vulgarest is as good as any. About the whole phenomenon everything has been said and nothing has been said. Yet this morning, with the miracle once again before my eyes, I am driven to say at least one thing more: to wonder whether anyone has ever dwelt sufficiently upon the strange fact that one of the most abundant substances this earth knows is also one of the most finely finished in the microscopic detail of each individual crystal.

Dirt itself is not so cheap as snow and very far from being so impermanent. Snow is made tonight to be dissolved into water again next month, or perhaps even next day. And yet each individual grain, billions upon billions upon billions of them, is finished perfectly as one or another of the hundreds of different six-pointed stars; as though each, instead of being piled in unnoticed, uncounted heaps, had been formed for the careful eye of some connoisseur with a lens. Surely there is nothing else in Nature which demonstrates more abundantly her profusion, the careless extravagance of her inexhaustible ability endlessly to create the beautiful.

And how quietly the flakes fall, either one by one or collected into soft, harmless-seeming masses. You would never suspect that anything so small and so soft could ever become formidable. You cannot even feel the weight of one flake on your cheek—only the tiny point of coldness when it touches and the tiny point of wetness as it melts. Yet the relentless accumulation of the individually imperceptible adds up to a crushing weight. At last the great limb of the elm or the maple comes down, or the backbone of the barn cracks. Talk about the last straw that breaks the camel's back! Why should we import so strange a metaphor from so distant a land? Does anyone, for that matter, even in Arabia, pile straws one by one upon a beast's complaining back? A snowflake is far lighter than any straw, yet right here in New England we see, every winter, one added to one until something gives way. "It was the last flake that broke Farmer Brown's rooftree" would be a far better expression.

Perhaps none of the other grand natural phenomena —certainly not the various kinds of rain—occurs in such a variety of ways as the snow, which comes either crystal by crystal or in fluffy masses. It drops imperceptibly to the ground or is driven by wind, and in the end it amounts to anything from a mere frosting on the dark earth to an accumulation burying every recognizable landmark. And whenever it takes itself seriously, whenever it really settles down to business, it is a paralyzing fact which demands, as no other routine phenomenon does, that we bow to its requirements. Only the great unexpected catastrophes, only flood and hurricane and fire, reduce us to such impotence, so defy us to deal adequately with them. And a catastrophe it would be on the scale of a flood or hurricane if we had to deal with it as we have to deal with them. Whole cities are buried, whole areas rendered almost untraversable. We could not possibly do anything about the ruin that has been piled upon us. Not forty maids with forty brooms, not forty times forty bulldozers or plows could do more than clear paths. And then, one day, it removes itself as silently as it had fallen, sinking down into the fields it had blanketed or trickling off in cold little streams. Where are the snows of yesteryear? It is with difficulty that they are even remembered. In August they did not seem possible; we hardly believe that they ever were.

The summer woods or the summer fields seem to tolerate, if not actually invite, man's intrusion. The trees, the shrubs, and the herbs are his green brothers, his allies in the struggle to make the earth live. But snow, so coldly and so inhumanly beautiful, seems a counterattack from the inanimate, an effort to wrest this globe from the things which live and to return it to its place among the lifeless celestial spheres, one of which it presumably once was. Perhaps that is the deepest reason why all our attempts to deal with it, either on a small scale or a large, are so ridiculously inadequate. What clumsy, Neanderthal devices boots and rubbers are; how we flounder about when in desperation we adopt them! Even in cities, where men are accustomed to consider themselves immune from the intrusions of mere Nature, the costliest and largest machines are grotesquely inefficient, and can do no more than barely establish a limping *modus vivendi* for the cities' inhabitants. Even in this time which proudly calls itself "the age of the automobile," the shiniest, the sleekest, and the most powerful motorcar slithers to a standstill on a road where the snow has only begun to accumulate. Even the engineers who have invented television and radar have been able to devise nothing better than that mockery, the skid-chain, which is a good deal less adequate for its purpose than the cave-man's stone ax was.

Perhaps it is this same utterly alien character which is also responsible for the fact that of all natural beauties, the beauty of snow is the one which man's touch most inevitably destroys. There is nothing he can do to it or with it which does not make it, even in his eyes, less beautiful rather than more. In the cities where it is only in the way, it is soon reduced to sheer ugliness. Even in the country, where a freshly plowed road looks only a little less attractive than the drifts themselves and where a well-shoveled path has a certain intimate appeal, the roadsides soon begin to look dingy, and the path, if much walked upon, begins to be untidy. Perhaps the delicate trace of a mouse's track across a virgin expanse adds a charm of its own, but it is a charm which carries the suggestion of a different world. Where man has so much as walked more than once, the perfection is marred. Snow is pre-eminently a natural beauty which is best when left alone.

I, for one, am sorry that we are compelled to resist it as much as we do. I am glad to have the roads plowed, but that is only because, as my life is arranged, I cannot simply stay where I am, as I should prefer to do. I think that in some ways it must have been better in former times, when those who lived in regions where the snow came as it comes here made no effort to keep the roads open. Even from the standpoint of mere convenience, it would seem better not to try to disregard this temporary blocking of the arteries of communication when we are as unsuccessful in our efforts as we really are. And from another standpoint, the case against "getting out" or "going anywhere" seems even stronger. Surely the real meaning, the real impressiveness of snow, is best appreciated when we yield to it as the animals do and, like some of them, lay up stores for the siege. To stay a week, perhaps, within my own doors, and to look out from my own windows upon a world made temporarily unexploitable by man, would have many of the advantages of what the religious call "a retreat." And I never struggle getting my car out of the garage in a storm that I do not glance shamefacedly up at one of those leaf-balls in a tree where some squirrel is comfortably biding his time. Did I or did I not hear a scornful laugh?

This is the time for solitude—best of all, for a *solitude à deux*. The snow itself is lonely or, if you prefer, self-sufficient. There is no other time when the whole world seems composed of one thing and one thing only. Here is no variety except the variety of form. The smooth, undulating expanses soothe but do not distract. How much, they seem to ask, do you have in yourself? What happens to you if you are not diverted? What is the winter of your own soul like? "The One remains, the many change and pass." Summer lies under the many-colored dome. Is this, perhaps, the white radiance of eternity?

Such questions may be asked even as one looks from a window, but the clearest answers come, or seem to come, during a walk in the moonlight though it be only along a recently plowed and now deserted road. Snow may sparkle gaily in the sunshine, but sunshine is the presence of our friend and the snow's enemy, the presence of something which carries the assurance that what looks as though it might endure forever will also pass away, that Nature has not really, as she seems, come to a point of rest which change will never again disturb. Such a sun is, like the rainbow, a covenant in the heavens.

As for dull skies, on the other hand, they can make even snow itself seem almost dull. But moonlight and snow are perfect complements, one to the other. There is sparkle now but it is a cold sparkle in light almost as colorless as the snow itself; light without heat, light from which the red of life is almost entirely absent. The earthly and the lunar landscapes no longer contrast. Essentially similar, they face one another across intervening space; the cold blue silver moon looking down upon us, and the cold blue silver earth looking back at it. We are alone, not only with Nature but with a Nature that seems to have ceased to breathe or to live.

Every man not completely devoid of imagination has, I suppose, at one time or another been overtaken by the fancy that he, or perhaps he and the companion who is alone with him, are the last persons to remain on this earth where all the others have died, or from which they have, still more terrifyingly, simply disappeared. It must be a fancy as nearly universal as dreams of falling or of flying and perhaps it is as ancient as human history. If the notion strikes us when we are alone or with a small company in the summer woods, it may take on the cheerful cast of the season itself and seem to promise almost infinite adventures as a sort of super Crusoe or as member of some uniquely fortunate Swiss Family Robinson. But moonlight and snow give it a very different complexion and there is one set of circumstances which induce it even more certainly than an evening walk.

Let the man who boasts that his common sense is continuous and unassailable arise about three or four o'clock on some snowy morning when there is a moon still up. I shall not recommend that he go out of doors; certainly not that he move even a few steps from his house; for I do not want to answer for the consequences if he should do any such thing. But let him simply look from his bedroom window at the waning moon about to set in the west. A waning moon it will be if there is any moon at all at that time in that position, and it will have a quality of its own. I do not know why this should be; especially not why (in my experience at least) it has always had a sullen, dark-copper glow rather than a silvery one. Perhaps the fact that only on those—for most of us—rather rare occasions when we are about at that hour do we ever see the moon with its illuminated side facing that direction in that part of the sky has something to do with the effect of strangeness, the vague sense that the phenomenon is somehow unnatural, as though one of the heavenly bodies had gone astray.

On our moonlight walk we take for granted that it was thoughtfully put there in the sky "to give a light by night." But who is, or should be, abroad at the dead hour of four? The moon is there, either for some purpose of her own or for no purpose at all. The heavenly machine is going through its changeless changes even while we sleep. There is certainly no lonesomer hour and no more eerie sight. A dead, white earth; a perfect stillness; and a strange, abnormal moon. At such a moment anything might happen. Or, what may seem even worse, nothing at all might happen—ever again.

January

God's Great Owl

The end of January is almost in sight now and for a full month the snow has been with us. As so often—though not always—it did not begin in earnest until Christmas was near, as though it had been waiting for the solstice when astronomical winter officially arrives. But once it *did* begin, it continued. Sometimes the first snow melts, and there is a bare season before the earth is covered again. This year when it came, it came to stay. Storms have followed one another at less than weekly intervals and one contribution has been added to another. There was a layer of separate, glittering crystals; then a layer of soft, fluffy, conglomerate flakes; then another of hard powder. The sun has never been

January

warm enough to melt even the surface and so, except in very exposed places, there is no icy glaze—only the dry, friable powder.

This snow, then, has been with us long enough so that it is now no novelty, but one of the conditions of a way of life. When it first fell it was exciting; as exciting almost as the first flowers of spring. Even my cats, I noticed, took it as gaily as children and dogs commonly do. As though they could not believe their eyes, they dashed about in the inch-high accumulation, pushing it before them on outstretched paws, or digging unnecessary little holes which the fluffy stuff made delightfully easy. Somewhat later, when communication paths two feet or more deep were first dug, they raced to and fro in them, with tails held straight in the air, delighted with the novelty. But to them, as to us, the snow has become only something to be lived with. Now they rarely leave the paths, which are become purely utilitarian. They walk in them only to get somewhere and they walk sedately, with tails down, not up. They know where unwary field mice can be caught, and though, like us, they act as if things would never be any different, they show plainly enough that the change since last summer seems decidedly for the worse.

I have often wondered whether they can remember that things were once different and whether they, also, assume that things will change again. Or do they live only in a series of moments, each of which is for them a separate "forever"? That they can recognize a once familiar situation when it recurs, I know, for I have seen them take up immediately some game they had learned to play the year before, and with the objects that suggest it. But how much they can spontaneously recall without some physical presences to start a reaction, I do not know. What do they think of as they lie by the fire between sleep and waking? Do they form images from the past or are they (as Mr. T. S. Eliot has declared) meditating with deep satisfaction on their secret names which, unlike the Navajos, they do not reveal to even their most intimate friends? And when they twitch in their sleep, are they dreaming as we dream?

To this last question your ultrabehaviorist prefers positively to say "no," but I do not see how he can be so sure. We should not believe that other human beings had any conscious life if we were not aware of our own, and if we did not, by analogy, attribute the same awareness to others. For all any of us know positively, each may be the only creature in the universe who is not an unconscious automaton. And if we *do* assume that another human being acts like us for the reason that he feels what we feel, it seems a violation of common sense not to assume, in the absence of any proof to the contrary, that the animals also have some thoughts and some feelings that accompany their actions. The evidence that a cat can dream seems to me almost as good as the evidence that anyone not myself has ever done so.

If I go for a walk either in daylight or in moonlight, the cats usually want to go with me. They start off on their own much less often than at other seasons but they recognize the signs of an impending sortie. They wait patiently, if somewhat condescendingly, while I— or, more often, their mistress and I—put on galoshes and wraps. Then we all sally forth together. Occasionally they will not return when we do; occasionally they will announce definitely that they think we have gone far enough. Usually, however, they seem perfectly content to let us set the limits, and they seem clearly to understand that the expedition has no specific object or goal; that in winter one walks for exercise and for large observation, but chiefly because the house feels so much better afterwards. Ordinarily they make no deviations from the path and they stop seldom to gaze or to sniff. To them, as to me, winter has turned the landscape into a kind of cold desert, where, as in the desert itself, the interest and the beauty do not lie in the thousand little details of summer but in mass, and surface, and form. The earth has been drastically simplified, and sweeping space is perhaps the most successful of its effects.

Even in New England, August creates what I assume to be a pretty good imitation of the jungle I have never seen; January certainly suggests the most wide-open and most arid regions of our own West, through which I have often wandered in automobile, on horseback, and afoot. Walking through snow a few inches deep is a good deal like walking through sand, and driving a car through a drift is even more like driving off the roads in New Mexico and Arizona. The same tricks will serve to negotiate what looks unnegotiable and they bring the same sense of triumph. The contrast between piercing cold and blazing heat is not sufficient to dispel the effect of similarity both in respect to mere physical form and, more importantly, in respect to a certain spiritual quality. Emptiness, loneliness, the sense that man is a mere accidental intruder, are as characteristic of the one as of the other.

The biologist might sum it up with inhuman detachment by saying that neither is an environment very favorable to life. But we are not, thank God, necessarily limited to analyses so detached that either winter or the desert need have no emotional significance, and "an environment not very favorable to life" may be translated into a sense of awe not untinged by fear. For that reason a desert or a winter landscape can be for us "sublime." Temporarily in the one, permanently in the other, the forces of death—or more properly the forces of the nonliving—have got the upper hand; and those of us, be we plants or animals or human beings, who have managed to survive have managed only by taking the

most elaborate precautions. In winter we wrap ourselves up and lie low; in the desert, where no waiting
will ever be long enough to witness any change, the
permanent dwellers have adopted strange devices and
deformed themselves in strange ways so that they and
their kind may hang on a little longer, may continue to
live in regions which would need to be only a little
hotter or a little drier to defeat the last of life's in-
genuities.

There are some to whom winter and desert alike are
nothing except distasteful hardship. For them the one
cannot be over, nor the other got out of, soon enough.
And perhaps to feel either as awesome or sublime one
must have some power of entering into that aspect of
Nature, that intention one might almost say, of which
desert and winter are the freest embodiments. To be
part of summer one must feel a part of life, but to be part
of winter one must feel a part of something older than
life itself. Here is beauty which is more literally, or at
least more indubitably, its own excuse for being than
is even the beauty of a flower. Perhaps the last is really
only a flower's way of attracting an insect. Perhaps the
song of the bird is intended for the ears of another bird,
if not for ours. In one way or another, life is calling out
to life, and beauty's excuse for being is the other living
thing which will be in some way aware of it. But the
snowflake cannot be *intended* for anything. It serves
no purpose, it is not observed—not even by another

crystal of ice. It is proof that inanimate Nature, by the very physical laws of her being, creates comeliness and symmetry.

Thus winter serves to remind us that the world would be beautiful even though there were no consciousness, no awareness, which could ever acknowledge that it was. And if it be objected that to say this is only to play with words—since "the beautiful" is something that exists only in the human mind—then I can only answer that it all merely comes down to the same thing as the ancient question whether the fall of a tree would make a sound when there was no one there to hear it. Beauty would exist without an eye to see it in precisely the same degree and precisely the same way that sound would exist even though there were no ear it could fall upon.

Traditionally—and properly—winter is for human beings the season of festivities. In the very middle of it are "the holidays," when we become gay by acting as though we were, and when there is something defiantly human about the deliberate, conscious triviality of the Christmas tree which substitutes for beauty the most childish kind of prettiness, as if we were determined to show what we can do in the way of frivolous decoration at the very time when Nature renounces everything of the sort. On these festive occasions we make sorties into the out-of-doors but they are sorties

only from which we return from the world we did not
make to the world of artificial light and artificial heat
which we have made for ourselves. No time is "cozier,"
but coziness means the sense of successful withdrawal
from the great world into a little one of our own.

Summer knows no such contrasts. We open wide the
windows and the doors to let the outside in. In the
country, at least, we abolish as far as possible the distinction between the two. The lawn is a drawing-room,
the woods a conservatory. There is no change of mood
as we move from the indoors to the out. Nature and we
are in the same frame of mind, we speak the same lan-
guage. But in January there is much more than the
mere physical chill to which we must adjust ourselves
when we leave the fireside. It is almost literally like
being transplanted to the moon where we must learn
to appreciate a new kind of landscape.

All about us now is beauty in its most inhuman form,
or at least its most completely nonhuman. History is
not ancient enough to tell us when mankind first discovered that smiling fields make glad the heart, but it
is within the period of the more recent recorded time
that Western civilization began generally to recognize
as beautiful the more awesome aspects of Nature; and
ice or snow must have waited even longer than mountains to be celebrated in prose or verse. In winter it is
the sublime which takes over, and the sublime is something which requires for its appreciation more detach-

ment than the very young or the very simple find it easy to achieve.

There is nothing else in Nature which seems so pure as a winter landscape and there is a curiously complex set of ideas connected with that adjective when it is so applied. A snowscape is white of course, and of course white is the universal symbol of "purity." But its beauty is also a matter of "pure" form, without color and without accent. Most important of all, perhaps, it is "pure" after a fashion peculiar to that which is not alive, since all life is "impure" both in the sense of being mixed and in the sense of being warm in various ways, including the sexual. Passions imply movement and movement implies change, the breaking of the line, the shifting of the form. Only what is not alive can be in so many different fashions "pure."

Surely, too, it is curious that what is actually one of the most transient things in Nature, the one that vanishes like a dream and leaves nothing behind, should also be the one which most strongly suggests permanence. For when the earth is covered with snow it looks as though it had come to rest at last; as though these stretches and these hillocks were as enduring as granite. It is almost as though Nature were exhibiting to us for a few brief weeks what eternity will be like.

I am, I think, rather less a transcendentalist than even the average man is. No voice has ever spoken to me in unmistakable, unambiguous terms. I have never simply "felt" that anything was and must be absolutely true. Neither have I ever believed in the authenticity of the communications which others are convinced that they have received from some source beyond humanity and beyond Nature. A stubborn rationality has always had for me the last word. There are, I say, far too many instances when the mechanism is obvious for me not to suspect that some all-too-human mental quirk is responsible for what I tend to regard as only less gross examples of self-deception. Awake or asleep, I insist, you dreamed. It was you who spoke to yourself, not something outside which addressed itself to you.

I must confess, however, that silence, and solitude, and snow, provide the conditions under which I come closest to feeling myself open to transcendental communication. I am not, mind you, speaking now of nothing more than the sense of intimacy with living things, the sense of being in the same fellowship with them. That is, to me, no more transcendental than friendship or human sympathy. It is merely an extension of that solidarity with one's own kind which very few indeed have never felt at least in connection with some members of their family or of their immediate circle of associates. It is based upon an identity of fundamental interests with what is essentially like one's self and it is either purely rational or but little beyond rationality. What I do mean is the half conviction that one has been spoken to by, or that one has to some extent penetrated into the meaning of, something which is neither the self nor anything like the self. And there is no time when one seems so surrounded by or so immersed in that which is not even remotely like the self as when one is out alone in a night of snow.

He who would feel the earth spin and the planets circle must get away from human beings and all other living things; even from whatever suggests them. Just as in human company one can hardly be properly aware of the other manifestations of animate Nature, so in the presence of animate Nature herself one cannot properly be aware of what is older and perhaps more enduring than animate Nature; with what was before her and will perhaps continue to be, time without end, after the last restless protozoan is dead and the last lichen shriveled on the surviving rock. It should not be on a night of storm, for that is something which must be struggled against and resistance to anything is fatal. But if it be a night of quiet and moonlight and snow, the physical place need not be remote. All the worlds except the white, dead, gleaming one can disappear twenty-five feet from a warm, cozy house.

I remember very vividly one such evening. It was the unghostly hour of eight P.M. and I had gone down the path shoveled across my lawn toward the garage, only a few dozen yards away. Suddenly I was alone with the universe. The realest things besides myself in all existence were not either human beings nor any other living things. I seemed about to grasp what the earth, the suns, and the stars meant to themselves as distinguished from what they mean to any of us creatures—from the simplest to the most complex—who live and grow and then die; who seem to have to purchase our kind of awareness at the price of the agreement that it shall be brief.

Then, at that very moment, came the far-away hoot—bark, it had better be called—of one of the great owls. There are few lonesomer sounds made by any living thing, but no living thing can be lonesome as the stars and the snow are lonesome. I remembered once having heard that the owl hoots in order to frighten the cowering mice into betraying by a start their secret whereabouts. What I saw now in my mind's eye was the sudden pounce of the great bird, the shrill scream of the mouse, and then—after aggressor and victim had disappeared together—the tiny spot of blood staining the inhuman purity of the snow. In an instant I was back among my own kind. The communication from space was never received. Sometimes I wonder whether God, the only time He ever began to speak to me, was interrupted by one of His own owls.

February

The One We Could Do Without

The most serious charge which can be brought against New England is not Puritanism but February. It is true that before we are finished with it the days are unmistakably longer than they were in December or January, and true that there are periods when the daylight is brighter, as well as longer. But these brief interludes are too infrequent to be counted on, and the relapses are so complete that the interludes do not seem even promises. Now more than ever one must remind oneself that it is wasteful folly to wish that time would pass, or—as the puritanical old saying used to have it—to kill time until time kills you. Spring is too far away to comfort even by anticipation, and winter long ago lost the charm of novelty. This is the very three A.M. of the calendar.

February

I will not say that I would like to dispense with February, for I should not willingly agree to make my life one-twelfth shorter—not even, I suppose, if it were going to be February all the year round. Nevertheless there are regions of the earth where the months bear the same names as ours but where the allotment of time to the various seasons has been more sensibly managed. Some of them, for instance, have a real November (in December), and a real December (in January), and then get on immediately to an April. That seems to me about right, and I would gladly exchange our February for another May; or, if that is asking too much, then for another October; or for, indeed, almost anything else I was offered. There are some optimists who search eagerly for the skunk cabbage which in February sometimes pushes itself up through the ice, and who call it a sign of spring. I wish that I could feel that way about it, but I do not. The truth of the matter, to me, is simply that skunk cabbage blooms in the winter time. There is no more cold-blooded animal than your frog, and you will not catch him stirring now.

On the western plains, so they say, the elk and the bison are growing lean and shaggy. Many of them die of exhaustion; others, which just manage to pull through, could not have done so if the winter had been even one week longer. No doubt it was during this month that the first animal first thought of the desperate device of hibernation, and one needs the soul of a chickadee not to have moments when one wonders if it would not be a good idea to sleep the month away.

Unmistakably the solstice has passed, the sun is climbing slowly higher, but we are paying now for that lag in the seasons which we enjoyed in the autumn. Death lingers as life did before. Indeed, in our latitude February snow can be the worst of the year; sometimes because it is actually the heaviest, sometimes because it is most likely to come mixed with sleet and freezing rain. This is the time when those—and I am one of them —who say that they would not care for the climates where there are no changes of season avoid bringing up that subject. Thank goodness, February is the shortest month, and somehow it is impossible, all rationality aside, not to blame leap year when it brings us one more day of it.

The very ancient Romans had no such month, and the learned say that it was introduced into the calendar by Numa Pompilius. These same learned say also that the name is from *februare*—to expiate—and that is certainly appropriate enough. Writing in the antique style, Ezra Pound celebrated the season with these lines:

> Skiddeth bus and sloppeth us,
> An ague hath my ham.
> Freezeth river, turneth liver,
> Damn you sing: Goddamm.

"If winter comes . . ." indubitably implies a fact of chronology well tested by experience. But I know few other instances where a major poet fails so conspicuously to carry emotional, as opposed to merely intellectual, conviction.

Even in the country those of us who unfortunately must leave it from time to time skid and slop in our cars, and I find that my pets share the general irritated discouragement. The cats meow at me as though they were asking that I do something about it all—not, I think, because they really believe me omnipotent, but because they are not sure just where my powers stop, and because cats seem to go on the principle that it never does any harm to ask for what you want. All winter, up until now, my ducks have waddled out of their night quarters to stand disconsolately around their frozen pool. For days on end in February they refuse to budge or to stick so much as the tip of a beak out of doors, and my goose obviously regrets that she did not accept the invitation of her wild fellows who, last fall, stopped the night near her and in the morning honked an invitation as they rose to resume their journey south.

Only one noteworthy event has so far occurred during the whole month; namely, an encounter between the boldest of my cats and a fox. The latter had approached one evening to within ten or twelve yards of the house and obviously the cat regarded him as no more than an intruding cur. Conscious that right was on his side, the cat made a bold attack and the fox ran yipping away into the darkness. What he thought the cat was, I do not know, but quite possibly this was, on his side, no case of mistaken identity. A cat out after an obviously unauthorized trespasser is nothing to be taken lightly.

Personally I had been glad enough to have the fox about, but I have found from experience that these things are not easy to explain. Indeed, though the cats know well enough that domesticated animals are not to be annoyed and though they accept the situation, they obviously think of themselves as like us rather than like the other pets, and they have scant affection for the lower animals. I am sure that one of them has often remarked to the other: "The only thing I don't understand about Him (and I am not really certain that he capitalizes me) is His absurd liking for animals."

This ability of some four- and even some two-legged creatures to join the human community and to reject, in greater or lesser degree, their own is one of the most astonishing things about them. It is something which goes far beyond mere taming, which is negative, and which becomes a positive identification. Dogs and cats, of course, do it more completely than any of the other animals met with in households and—popular prejudice notwithstanding—cats as completely as dogs, though they lack the dog's willingness to do anything, understandable or not, for no other reason than the fact that The Master would like it. Both want to participate in purely human activities; both are saddened when they are denied, either by human insistence or by their own limitations, the privilege of doing so. I can well believe the account given by an experimenter who raised an ape child with a human one. For many months the ape kept well in advance of the child; was plainly the brighter of the two. And when the time came that he began to fall behind, he was obviously distressed until at last a sort of confirmed melancholy settled upon him. Something in his eyes seemed to reveal his awareness that he was not, as he had formerly supposed, going to become a man in the end. Perhaps that is a point in favor of the Lamarckians.

But cats, dogs, and apes are not the only creatures who can actually be changed by association with human beings. Even barnyard fowls—the goose more conspicuously than any other—behave differently; they get, especially, a different look about the eyes and lose a certain blankness of expression characteristic of those that have associated with only their own kind. Speech is the great civilizer and just listening to what is only vaguely comprehended as an attempt at communication, does something to even a small brain.

Chickens are among the most notable examples of the animals whom domestication has made less rather than more than what a wild animal is, but that is because the chicken has been a victim of pure exploitation and only rarely taken into the human community. Yet even a chicken, brought up where there are only a few of his kind and allowed to peck about the doorway, is noticeably different from the product of one of those factories where Nature is persuaded to go in for mass production. Who that has ever read the passage can forget Thoreau's description of an Irishman's kitchen where a hen wandered about "looking too humanized to roast well?"

That any animal ever proceeded so far as to learn the dubious art of looking before and after, I am by no means sure. None of mine has given me any intimation that he knows that February is other than a permanent condition, and of course it is impossible to know whether or not those wild creatures who, last fall, prepared for winter had any conception of why it was advisable to do what they did. But if animals are deprived of hope (as well as of fear), they are compensated by being given an almost endless patience for enduring, or simply for waiting.

And as usual it is the cats who are provided with the most perfect mechanism. They are, to be sure, capable of a kind of short-range impatience—when, for example, food is being prepared. They seem at times to suffer momentarily from boredom, as a wild animal perhaps never does. But when the weather is too bad to go out, or when for any reason there is absolutely nothing to do, they can simply curl up and sleep almost endlessly, for days at a time if necessary, with perfect ease. Even going to sleep seems to be a process entirely under their control, as voluntary as shutting the eyes is for us. Cats are rather delicate creatures and they are subject to a good many different ailments, but I never heard of one who suffered from insomnia.

Of course different species of animals differ not only in the extent to which they readily become humanized but also in the hold which the human community has when some stimulus from the wild reaches them. Notoriously the pet crow, teachable though he is and delighted though he seems to be with human activities, will often join his fellows in the fall. The cat can sometimes go wild—though not by any means so easily, so willingly, or so successfully as those who abandon pets sometimes like to tell themselves. And in my experience the goose—whom the ancient Romans regarded much as we regard the dog, and would never never have been so foolish as to use for a symbol of foolishness—takes to human association as no nother barnyard animal does. W. H. Hudson thought it the most intelligent bird that man had ever had intimate association with, and perhaps he was right.

Your duck, on the other hand, though he likes to be talked to if he has no companions of his own, very easily forgets human association, as I had occasion recently to observe in the case of a long-established pet. At the age of twelve she (as the saying is) "became a mother for the first time" and immediately, in a frenzy of maternal solicitude, insisted upon regarding all human beings as potential enemies. Neither a cat nor a dog, of course, would have made any such mistake. Either would ask and expect to get protection from any person previously known to be well disposed. But this particular duck's faith in the creatures who had looked after her for a dozen long years was obviously very tenuous. At any approach she would go into an insane dither of excitement and attack anyone in sight. In fact, her emotional tumult was so great that she would forget whom she was mad at and presently begin to maul the ducklings themselves so ferociously that I had to keep away for fear she would kill them instead of me. Whether this confused tendency to take anger out on whoever was nearest at hand is to be regarded as animal dullness or as the exhibition of a distinctly human trait, I will leave an open question.

To anyone who did not know him, Thoreau's "too humanized to roast well" might possibly suggest brutality, or at least a tendency to regard animals as mere walking dinners. As a matter of fact he was, of course, almost a vegetarian, and though I am not that, I certainly share the common—and not very logical—human refusal to eat any fellow creatures who were not strangers to me in life. Certainly, to dine off a fowl that had once listened, even dimly, to a conversation addressed to it would be a kind of cannibalism, and I was never able to eat the eggs of my pet goose—not because it would be cruel but because it would have seemed indecently intimate.

They say that when one of Tolstoi's acquaintances, who happened to be a bigoted meat-eater, came to dinner, he found a chicken and a knife tied to the table leg; if he wanted meat, Tolstoi told him, he would have to prepare it himself. If this were the universal custom, I imagine that a great many animal lives would be saved. That division of labor which is responsible for the profession of butcher is one of the most important single factors against which the vegetarian has to contend. There is more than one kind of dirty work which we habitually hire others to do for us.

Many different men have rationalized in many different ways their decision to disregard the scruples they could not help feeling. Benjamin Franklin, for instance, was a vegetarian for a while until he happened to see a fish being cleaned and observed a smaller fish removed from its belly. If, he said to himself, the fish can eat other fish, then I can eat him. And if Franklin really meant that whatever is permitted to any living creature is permissible to man also, he was following Nature with a vengeance.

Personally I like somewhat better—for its ingenuity at least—the excuse trumped up by that eighteenth-century educator, sociologist, Rousseauist, and general crank, Thomas Day. He argued that, so far as the domestic animals are concerned, we do not deprive them of life but actually confer it, since if we did not raise pigs to eat, there would indeed be few if any pigs in all the world, and thus we do not deprive them of their old age but rather give them their youth. This, although Day was presumably unaware of the fact, is positively Thomistic, for it assumes that man's creation of pigs, like God's creation of man, is an act of Generosity, not of Justice. The pig has no right to complain against the butcher's knife. He should be grateful that he ever had the privilege of living at all.

If Franklin's argument is a little too simple for me, Thomas Day's is a bit too subtle, and in actual fact the excuse I offer myself is only a somewhat more guarded version of Poor Richard's. Your animal, says the biologist, is by biological necessity a "compulsory protein feeder"—compulsory, you will please note, to distinguish him from such carnivorous plants as the sundew, which consume protein in the form of insects captured on the natural fly-paper they use for leaves, but which can get along without it. Once the animal parted company with the plant, once he decided to become animal rather than vegetable, he was committed to the consumption of things that have life. And though it is true that he can survive on plant life alone, even this involves killing, or at least exploitation; and it is only one step from the murder of a cabbage to the murder of a fish. This is one of the ineluctable contingencies of the natural universe, a part of the world I never made; the

---

lion cannot lie down with the lamb without ceasing to be a lion, for he would soon fall a victim to starvation and thus cease to be anything at all.

If we are going to resist Nature—and I agree that some resistance to her dictates is the minimum price we must pay to remain human at all—we must begin with things less central. There are many natural tendencies we have still to combat successfully before we tackle anything so fundamental as the facts that we are "compulsory protein feeders," and that animal flesh is a rich source which it is beyond most human wills to resist. In February, especially, these arguments seem very persuasive, and I find myself reading vegetarian propaganda less sympathetically than the writings of that almost unique proponent of an exclusive meat diet, Vilhjalmur Stefansson. In his experience, he says, no one who has ever eaten nothing but frozen caribou meat three times a day for a month or two wants to eat anything else, ever.

As I have been writing these pages the month has been passing. On the twenty-first of December, through the crudest possible of homemade devices, I had sighted the setting sun from one of my windows and marked on the sill a line running toward that point on the horizon which is the point farthest south the sun, in this latitude, will ever touch. It was for a similar purpose —to mark the longest day—that the Druids set up the two tallest pillars in those stone circles which still stand, here and there, in England and in France; and when I drew my line I had the sense that I was but echoing them as I said: "Thus far shalt thou go and no farther." Perhaps both of us were to some extent victims of Chanticleer's delusion that what we signalize, we are responsible for.

Only yesterday I took my sights again, and even with my highly inaccurate device it was impossible to miss the fact that the sun had accomplished something in her struggle to return toward the north again. As the astrologers would have said, she was in the sign of Aquarius then, in the sign of Pisces now. And we won't go into the fact that, because of that delightfully esoteric phenomenon known as "the precession of the equinoxes," the sun nowadays is not really in Pisces until it is nominally in Aries. This is something that only the modern astrologers need to bother about—and something that (I am told) they do not.

Even as I write these lines, some clouds have parted and sunshine, as though to rebuke me for having singled this out as the most hopeless of months, is streaming down. But the snow on which it shines is as deep as ever. Almost the whole of the winter's accumulation is still there. And I know from experience how many false springs there will be before the real one comes. April may be the cruelest month, but March is certainly the most inconsistent.

March

An End and a Beginning

On the first of January nothing happens except to the calendar. The date marks no astronomical event and corresponds to no change in the seasons, either here or anywhere else. The ancient Jews, Egyptians, and Greeks—all of whom put the beginning of the new year in March instead—were following a sound instinct, and so were the Englishmen who for so long stubbornly refused to change their old custom. Perhaps the world was not actually created for the first time in March of 4004 B.C. (as Archbishop Ussher demonstrated to his own and many people's satisfaction), but March is when it is annually created anew, and that is when the calendar of the soul begins.

March

The Romans were the first to start with January as well as the first to give the month that name, and it was Julius Caesar who placed January 1st in its present position. They say that he would have preferred to begin—with at least astronomical logic—at the solstice, which occurs near December 21st. But the solstice happened to coincide too closely with the Saturnalia, and he doubted that his countrymen would be in a sufficiently clear state of mind to begin anything then. Accordingly he allowed them ten days in which to sober up, and placed the new year as close to the solstice as he dared after taking due account of the national hangover.

Was there ever a less poetical reason for any important decision? A fig for those Romans and their famous practicality! Because of them, one more link between man and Nature was broken; one more reminder that we are part of an All was obliterated. In our hearts those of us who know anything worth knowing know that in March a new year begins, and if we plan any new leaves, it will be when the rest of Nature is planning them too. I am not sure that I desire to begin a new life, but I am ready then to start the old one afresh.

A certain blind man knew that the seasons return even though they did not return for him, and that is more than most who have eyes can boast. They live by the calendar and they know the days of the week. This, they may be able to tell you, is Friday, March 5th. But the fact is merely arbitrary and arithmetical, part of a necessary arrangement for keeping track of their engagements—most of which they would rather forget—and of their obligations—most of which are a burden. It implies no awareness of either the stars in their courses or of the natural rhythms which they do not even know they share. Perhaps there is no better symbol than this of our deliberate withdrawal from any life not poverty-stricken so far as the basic emotions are concerned, and perhaps the calendar of the savage with its "Moon of the Hunt" and "Moon of the Rains" is better. Perhaps accuracy is too dearly purchased as the cost of such desiccation.

From another year which I hope will be based in the country—if not, alas, spent continuously there—I promise myself many advantages. But none of them is more obvious or more inclusive than the privilege of being permitted to be continuously aware that I am indeed alive—for that is a fact which the city makes most people forget, and which can be fully appreciated only by those whose own souls feel the ebb and flow of vital tides, who build their mansion on an inlet of the sea, not on some landlocked harbor which nowhere communicates with any deeper and vaster body. Only those within whose own consciousness the suns rise and set, the leaves burgeon and wither, can be said to be aware of what living is.

Perhaps all who have ever been in that way aware were aware of the same thing, no matter at what time they lived or of what civilization they were a part. Perhaps all the ceremonies and myths and poems connected with Nature (and that may include even science itself) are in their origins merely attempts to cultivate or to formulate such an awareness, though each tends to become, in its own way, a substitute for the very thing it was intended to promote; and one practices the ritual of the corn-dance or the microscope more and more stubbornly as it loses more and more of its meaning.

However that may be, the facts remain that the rituals do vary and that what men think or say about the relation between them and Nature changes so much even from generation to generation, and even within the same civilization, that poetry itself sometimes loses the meaning it had when it was written and sometimes, after such a lapse, reveals that meaning again at another time or place. Meanwhile new knowledge, new theories, and new beliefs tend to change the color or the form of the fundamental experiences without, perhaps, altering their essential character. And, since it is the form and color which can be most easily described or discussed, we have the sense of defining new attitudes even though all the description and the discussion are only attempts to win back the fundamental and the unutterable. The Druid built his Stonehenges, and I make my pencil-mark upon the window-sill.

Some argue that urban life has had less to do with our progressive alienation from Nature than has the increase of our knowledge. They say that it is not so much because we are physically isolated that Nature means less and less to most people as because, having come to know better and better what she is really like, we are less and less able to formulate the myths which interpret her in terms acceptable to us. But we are part of her, nevertheless, no matter what she may be; and we cannot renounce her merely because we know, or think we know, some of her darker secrets. Whatever we discover about her we are discovering also about ourselves.

She may not have—as in one historic burst of enthusiasm men seemed ready to proclaim—any "simple plan" which we need only to follow. Her "social union" is not the idyllic thing which some supposed it. There never was and perhaps there never will be any "Golden Age." But there is what there is, and it is something both stupendous and incredible. Not to be aware of it is to be to that shocking extent deaf, dumb, and blind—or, what is perhaps worse, to number oneself among those who have eyes but see not.

One may grant readily enough that to "love Nature" is not so easy as it seemed to the Rousseauists and the

Wordsworthians. Perhaps she is not in so simple or so bland a sense "lovable," or lovable only. Perhaps she has many dwellings, not all of which are as seemly as "the light of setting suns." Perhaps she is sometimes capable of betraying the heart that loved her. Perhaps (in other words) we have, from the Wordsworthian point of view, made the mistake of looking at her too closely and objectively; been too given to "peep and botanize," too little willing to rest content when we have found or believed we have found the "thoughts too deep for tears." Because of that fact, Nature is no longer merely a "social union," nor is she merely the source of "the picturesque" or even of "the sublime." In part at least she is also again what Thomas Hobbes called her: "the state of war"—and war is not sublimity, pure and uncontaminated.

Yet I am by no means sure that I would exchange the puzzle and the excitement of the Nature which science has helped us to see for the eighteenth century's mere illusory idyl. The woods and the fields—even the garden and the lawn—are not merely a soothing presence. They are a challenge to thought and a challenge to emotion. If we would accept the universe, then all this is part of what we must accept, and what goes on in these woods and these gardens is also some sort of clew to the universe in which we live. There is much still to be discovered, and possibly much more to which emotional adjustments will have to be made. For whether we delight to remember the fact or attempt to forget it, the contingencies of Nature have something to say about the contingencies of human nature also. To the fatuous remark that "life is strange" there was once retorted the knock-down question: "By comparison with what?" But was the remark, after all, really fatuous, or the question really knock-down? It is a fact that there is nothing with which Nature can be compared; and it is the fact that she is absolute that makes her absolutely strange.

We are still children of the nineteenth century, and that century is nothing more characteristically than it is the century which began to assume a sort of desperate attitude toward those problems of man and society which the eighteenth century had tended to regard as gradually but surely reaching a solution. Alexander Pope could proclaim that "Whatever is is right"; and if the most optimistic of Victorian poets seems to be saying the same thing with his "God's in His heaven," it is only a seeming, for Browning was proclaiming a paradox which was striking for the very reason that, to most of his contemporaries, it was so improbable a statement. The next most cheerful of English spokesmen could go no further than the mere hope that "somehow good will be the final goal of ill," and his rather fussy concern with what he disapproved of in Nature was far more characteristic of his age.

It is curious, also, that two nineteenth-century prose writers who in all probability never heard of each other should nevertheless have also expressed, each in his own way, not the assurance that knowledge would turn out to be just what we should prefer to find it, but the conviction that, no matter what the event, we can do nothing except pursue even the possibly unpalatable truth. Speaking for official science, Thomas Henry Huxley demanded that we should "follow Nature no matter to what black abyss she may lead." Speaking for himself and for whatever fellows he might find in his devotion to a less formal communion with Nature, Thoreau wrote in the last chapter of *Walden* a rather surprising sentence when he was urging his fellows to go in for the exploration of themselves rather than for geography, and then demanded: "What does Africa, what does the West stand for? Is not our own interior white on the chart? black though it may prove, like the coast, when discovered."

Huxley certainly had in mind those of his contemporaries who were afraid lest science should destroy the foundations of what they believed had now an exclusive right to be called Religion. Thoreau, I suppose, was addressing those of his Transcendentalist contemporaries who seemed too content to assume that Nature merely confirmed what they wanted to believe. Each in his own way and in terms appropriate to his own audience was reiterating the conviction that we cannot presume to tell Nature in advance what she should teach us, and each was issuing a warning against the too complacent belief that we shall always find the lesson palatable.

But if, rejecting such advice, we turn away from Nature, then to what shall we turn? Shall we devote ourselves to Man, to human nature exclusively? Or to God, conceived of as something outside Nature as well as outside Man?

Both recommendations have been made and some have professed to follow either the one or the other. But is there any human nature which is discontinuous—a thing-in-itself? If God should be found, could He turn out to be anything utterly different from His own manifestations? These are metaphysical questions, and very slippery ones. While they remain unanswered, mankind has unfortunately been giving a practical and terribly mistaken answer to the original question which provoked them.

What we have actually done as we have built cities and tended to lead more and more exclusively urban lives is not to turn toward either the God-who-is-not-Nature or the Man-who-is-not-Nature but to busy ourselves and identify ourselves with that part of the natural world which is not alive rather than with that part which is. What we have tended to become is not either the Humanist or the Worshiper but quite simply the mechanic and the technologist. We have forgotten the beast and the flower not in order to remember either ourselves or God, but in order to forget everything except the machine.

Man seems always to have insisted upon setting up for himself some sort of dichotomy; upon opposing one kind, or mode, or order of reality to another. Sometimes God is thought of as opposed to the Nature of which Man is a part; sometimes Nature is thought of as opposed to Man who is separate from it, though perhaps either related to, or a part of, God. But neither of these oppositions seems so obvious, so clear, or so immediately meaningful as the opposition between that part of Nature which lives and that part which does not.

Each of the two separate systems is vast, complicated, and wonderful. To be not alive does not mean to be inert or without organization. The planets dance in obedience to beautifully intricate laws, and the atoms do the same. In fact, it seems almost as though the nonliving were the more orderly, the more dependable of the two; as though life involved the introduction of the willful, the unpredictable, perhaps even of the random. It is a rebellion against law and probability, an intrusion—perhaps spontaneous and anarchical —into what would otherwise have been a system, perfect in its neatness and regularity. Perhaps it was only an accident, perhaps God Himself did not originally envisage it. Perhaps by now it is opposing itself even to Him. And if that is so, then it may be the most stupendously incomprehensible accident that ever happened since endless time began to run.

Under such a dichotomy there can never be any doubt where Man belongs. The bounds of any other categories are difficult to define. No one has ever been able to point to a clear line which separates the Human from the Natural, or the Natural from the Divine. But so far at least as our practical experience goes, we never meet any difficulty in recognizing that which is alive, and therefore like us. Your biochemist may be given pause by the ferments and the enzymes, may hesitate to classify them as either living or not-living; and it may possibly be true (as he sometimes suspects) that it was in some such substance as this that the Great Rebellion began. But the question is of no immediate practical importance so far as our lives are concerned. What we have to decide is merely whether we shall choose to have our chief business with the obviously living or the obviously not-living—and we have made the wrong choice.

We have chosen to have our most intimate association with machines, not with fellow creatures; to regard plants and animals as curiosities to be eliminated as far as is practicable from our own environment and relegated to museums, when they are not actually "liquidated." And we are indifferent to the fact that whereas cities can be rebuilt, whereas some man might conceivably repaint a lost Leonardo or rewrite a lost poem, the extinct animals—from the most insignificant insect to the noblest mammal—are genuinely what lost works of art are sometimes called: irrecoverable. Electronic calculators can solve problems which the man who made them cannot solve; but no government-subsidized commission of engineers and physicists could create a worm, because that tiny spark of rebellion is the thing which man shares with it but which he cannot call into being.

Late in the nineteenth century certain scientists began to ask whether dead nature was really dead, whether even the atoms merely obeyed the laws which were supposed to rule them. The philosopher Charles Sanders Peirce turned up with the strange fancy that perhaps the whole concept of "a law of nature" was false—that what we have to deal with is not atoms which always have "obeyed laws" but particles which have merely become fixed in the habit of behaving in a certain way, just as animals and men have fallen into certain habits so regular that an observer who saw only great masses of men might conclude that they necessarily obeyed laws—such as, for instance, the law that they flow in the direction of Coney Island on hot week ends.

The most casual reader of popular science is aware that modern physics tends in the direction of recognizing a "principle of indeterminacy," of assuming at the very least that the deadness of dead Nature does not involve all it was once supposed to involve. Possibly they are right. But that hardly changes the fact that though the dichotomy may ultimately break down and the Two become One, we are still more like the animal than like either the enzyme or the atom and are still making the mistake of not claiming the kinship. Perhaps, indeed, the tendency to find some faint evidence of life in what is ordinarily called dead is actually the expression of an uneasiness, a desperate attempt to make less utterly alien that half of the universe to which we have already committed ourselves. Perhaps no race not aware that it had denied the fellowship obviously open to it would be interested in attributing such tenuous life to such intangible objects as atoms.

The danger is that man himself may go on becoming more and more like the machines with which he lives, that his thoughts will grow colder and colder and his emotions weaker and weaker as he alienates himself farther and farther from everything in the universe which is capable of any kind of warmth. Is it merely an accident that the large-scale cruelties are usually practiced in the name of Religion or the name of Science? Is it merely an accident, or is it the result of the fact that both Religion and Science tend to belittle as "sentimental" and misleading that mere sympathy with other living creatures, human or nonhuman, which is the source of all compassion? Religion sets up the soul as a barrier between man and the animals and makes a similar distinction between the man who is saved and the man who is not; Science sets up a barrier between what is logical and what is not; but the results can be curiously similar. Burn him because he is theologically wrong; "liquidate him" because the science of politics proves that he is opposing the greatest happiness of the greatest number! Man professes to try to be human partly because he would avoid the uncomprehending cruelty of the cat, but he has been ill-advised if that has entailed adopting the grand cruelty of the Inquisitor or the Commissar. Whenever man forgets that man is an animal, the result is always to make him less humane.

Against anything so vast as the whole tendency of a civilization to move away from Nature, to forget its origins and to cut off its deepest roots, there may seem to be little effective that can be done, and perhaps indeed nothing can be done. Urbanization and mechanization are themselves only symptoms of something deeper, proofs of how far we have proceeded along a road which may have branched away from another possible one so long ago that there is no retracing of our steps. If I choose to live as much of my life as possible just beyond the city's outermost limits, if I observe my woods and cultivate the friendship of my pets, even if I think sometimes that I have established some sort of communication with life itself, I hardly suppose that I am thereby going to reverse a trend or point the way to salvation for the human race. Perhaps I can hardly suppose that I am, at most, doing any more than glancing back over my shoulder as I am carried forward by a race most members of which do not take the time to do even that. Perhaps I am merely straining my ears to hear the last faint sounds of a receding music which, soon, no one will ever again hear at all. If so, then so be it. It is something to have been able to do even that.

At least I am glad to know that this is March, am glad that I know it as phenomena observed and as something felt in my own bones, not merely as something I read on my calendar. I have been living through a year, not merely existing in an abstraction called time. The year has meant to me participation in a cycle, the awareness of an ebb and flow, of being part of a vital and complex process. To me July and August, January and February, have been epochs, each with a character of its own; seasons during which appropriate business was done by me and by hundreds of other creatures fascinatingly like and fascinatingly unlike what I am. At this moment I am standing on the threshold of a new year waiting to begin a new cycle of months forever familiar and forever new. "Seasons return"—though sooner or later each of us must add: "but not for me."

So far there has been no sign of the revival that I know will soon be here. In a week, in two weeks, in three or four at the most, I shall some night hear all about me the shrill piping from the ponds, and I shall know that the first voice to celebrate the return of warmer days has begun its jubilation.

Hyla crucifer is what the biologists call him, but to most of us he is simply the Spring Peeper. . . .

Da Capo